POCKETFUL OF

Bible

P

GRADUATES

DaySpring

LIVE YOUR FAITH

Pocketful of Bible Promises for Graduates
© 2018 DaySpring Cards, Inc. All rights reserved.
First Edition, March 2019

Published by:

P.O. Box 1010
Siloam Springs, AR 72761
dayspring.com

Bible Translations Used:

CEV: Scriptures taken from the Contemporary English Version.
© 1991, 1992, 1995 by American Bible Society. Used by permission.

HCSB: Scripture taken from the Holman Christian Standard Bible®.
© 1999, 2000, 2002, 2003 by Holman Bible Publishers. Used by permission.

KJV: Scripture taken from the Holy Bible, King James Version.

NASB: Scripture from the NEW AMERICAN STANDARD BIBLE®,
© Copyright The Lockman Foundation. (www.lockman.org).

NCV: Scripture from the New Century Version®. Copyright © 2005 by Thomas
Nelson, Inc. Used by permission. All rights reserved.

NKJV: Scripture from the New King James Version. Copyright © 1982 by
Thomas Nelson, Inc.

NLT: Scripture quotations are taken from the Holy Bible, New Living
Translation, copyright © 1996, 2004, 2007 by Tyndale House Foundation. Used
by permission of Tyndale House Publishers, Inc., Carol Stream, Illinois 60188.
All rights reserved.

THE MESSAGE: Scripture quotations from The Message. © Eugene Peterson.
Permission from NavPress.

TLB: © The Living Bible. Taken from the Living Bible with permission from
Tyndale House Publishers, Inc., Wheaton, IL.

Prime: 91628
ISBN: 978-1-68408-680-1

CONTENTS

INTRODUCTION

C ongratulations, Graduate! You've hit a huge milestone. And this little book is here to encourage you as you set out on the next adventure the world has to offer! Are you worried? Excited? Trust the promises that God has made you. Do you have a difficult task ahead? Ask God for courage. Do you have too many new responsibilities that you're unsure how to handle? Ask God to help you prioritize your day and your life. Whatever your circumstance, whatever your need, God is enough. No challenges are too big for Him, not even yours.

The Bible is a book like no other. It is a gift from the Creator, a guidebook for life here on earth and a road map for eternal life. And it's a book of promises.

When God makes a promise, He keeps it. No exceptions. So the verses in this text are not hypotheticals; they're certainties. They apply to every generation, including yours, and they apply to every human being, including you.

1

ABIDING

*When the Holy Spirit controls our lives He will
produce this kind of fruit in us: love, joy, peace,
patience, kindness, goodness, faithfulness,
gentleness and self-control.*
GALATIANS 5:22–23 TLB

Chop a limb off a tree and it won't take long to
notice a difference in that limb. It will become
dry and broken, its leaves withered, and eventually
break down back into the earth.

Now graft a branch into a tree and you'll see a
difference too. When done correctly, a grafted branch
takes on the characteristics of the tree. It grows leaves
and blooms, bearing fruit, and in every way acting as
if it belonged to that tree from the beginning.

Jesus is the vine and we are the branches. We
have everything we need to bear much fruit in Him.
We just need to stay connected.

*God isn't into the rat race. He's into the slower
rhythms of life like dwelling, abiding, learning,
remembering, and being in His presence.*
LYSA TERKEURST, AUTHOR

GOD'S PROMISES
ABOUT ABIDING

Anyone who gets so progressive in his thinking that he walks out on the teaching of Christ, walks out on God. But whoever stays with the teaching, stays faithful to both the Father and the Son.
II JOHN 1:9 THE MESSAGE

And He has put His own Holy Spirit into our hearts as a proof to us that we are living with Him and He with us.
I JOHN 4:13 TLB

Dear children, remain in fellowship with Christ so that when He returns, you will be full of courage and not shrink back from Him in shame.
I JOHN 2:28 NLT

If you keep My commandments, you will abide in My love, just as I have kept My Father's commandments and abide in His love.
JOHN 15:10 NKJV

But if you remain in Me and My words remain in you, you may ask for anything you want, and it will be granted!
JOHN 15:7 NLT

2

ACCEPTANCE

*You didn't choose Me. I chose you. I appointed you to
go and produce lasting fruit, so that the Father will
give you whatever you ask for, using My name.*
JOHN 15:16 NLT

Ugh! You just got a speeding ticket. *Thank You,
Lord, for reminding me to stay safe.* The coffee
shop is out of that one drink you count on every day.
*Thank You for reminding me of what I can live with-
out.* You see a "C" on your report card for the first
time. *Thank You for challenging me to work through
difficult circumstances.*

Everything we face has kingdom value. It can all
be cashed in for treasure. And it's often the things
that seem the least special and wonderful that have
the greatest impact.

The next time you are inconvenienced in some
way, try being deliberate in giving thanks. It may
just change your outlook and make you feel richer in
Christ.

*Not being able to fully understand God is frustrating,
but it is ridiculous for us to think
that we have the right to limit God to something
we are capable of comprehending.*
FRANCIS CHAN, PASTOR

GOD'S PROMISES
ABOUT ACCEPTANCE

The trumpeters and singers performed together in
unison to praise and give thanks to the LORD.
II CHRONICLES 5:13 NLT

Your greatest glory will be that you belong to Him.
II THESSALONIANS 1:12 TLB

You are a chosen people. You are royal priests,
a holy nation, God's very own possession.
I PETER 2:9 NLT

Everything God created is good,
and to be received with thanks.
Nothing is to be sneered at and thrown out.
I TIMOTHY 4:4 THE MESSAGE

He is the LORD. He will do what He thinks is good.
I SAMUEL 3:18 HCSB

We don't yet see things clearly. We're squinting in a
fog, peering through a mist. But it won't be long before
the weather clears and the sun shines bright!
I CORINTHIANS 13:12 THE MESSAGE

3

ACCEPTING CHRIST

The Spirit of God, who raised Jesus from the dead,
lives in you. And just as God raised Christ Jesus from
the dead, He will give life to your mortal bodies by this
same Spirit living within you.
ROMANS 8:11 NLT

No one could ever accuse Jesus of being politically correct! He said some pretty controversial things in His day, which challenged people to either trust Him or turn away.

"If you eat my flesh and drink my blood..." *What?* Possibly the most head-turning statement ever!

"You're not sure you're ready to follow Me? If you turn back now to take care of business first, your heart is divided. No man who turns back can follow Me."

"My mother and brothers are here to see Me? That's nice. But my real mom and brothers are those who believe in Me."

A person tends to be either drawn in or pushed away by Jesus and who He is. God is true above all else, regardless of how that might appear to the rest of the world. And that's what makes Him so trustworthy.

God surpasses our dreams when we reach past our personal plans and agenda to grab the hand of Christ and walk the path He chose for us. He is obligated to keep us dissatisfied until we come to Him and His plan for complete satisfaction.

BETH MOORE, SPEAKER

GOD'S PROMISES ABOUT ACCEPTING CHRIST

For God loved the world so much that He gave His only Son so that anyone who believes in Him shall not perish but have eternal life.

JOHN 3:16 TLB

And this is the testimony: God has given us eternal life, and this life is in His Son. The one who has the Son has life. The one who doesn't have the Son of God does not have life.

I JOHN 5:11—12 HCSB

Work hard for sin your whole life and your pension is death. But God's gift is real life, eternal life, delivered by Jesus, our Master.

ROMANS 6:23 THE MESSAGE

I am the good shepherd. The good shepherd sacrifices His life for the sheep.

JOHN 10:11 NLT

4

ADVENTURE

God, who got you started in this spiritual adventure,
shares with us the life of His Son and our Master
Jesus. He will never give up on you. Never forget that.
I CORINTHIANS 1:9 The Message

In the book *The Secret Garden,* a young girl discovers a hidden passage in a wall. The passage leads to the most beautiful garden she has ever seen. And there she spends her days in wonder.

Following the Lord is like having Him lead you to secret passage after secret passage, into the most beautiful and unexpected places. Life could never be the same without Him.

It may seem convenient or simpler to do whatever feels good at the moment. But there's no simpler joy than to rest in God and let Him take you on His adventures.

The most difficult time in your life may be the border
to your promised land.
Christine Caine, activist

GOD'S PROMISES
ABOUT ADVENTURE

Keep traveling steadily along His pathway and in due season He will honor you with every blessing.
PSALM 37:34 TLB

You chart the path ahead of me and tell me where to stop and rest. Every moment You know where I am.
PSALM 139:3 TLB

What joy for those whose strength comes from the LORD, who have set their minds on a pilgrimage to Jerusalem.
PSALM 84:5 NLT

When the Holy Spirit, who is truth, comes, He shall guide you into all truth, for He will not be presenting His own ideas, but will be passing on to you what He has heard. He will tell you about the future.
JOHN 16:13 TLB

God, my shepherd! I don't need a thing.... Even when the way goes through Death Valley, I'm not afraid when you walk at my side. Your trusty shepherd's crook makes me feel secure.
PSALM 23:1, 4 THE MESSAGE

5

ADVERSITY

But He said to me, "My grace is sufficient for you,
for power is perfected in weakness."
II CORINTHIANS 12:9 HCSB

The most difficult circumstances are often the most effective ways for the Lord to get through to us. If we're willing to learn, He is willing to walk us to the other side of maturity and endurance and hope. Those who have been there know. It's hard to say "I would do that all over again" knowing how you've grown. But the truth is, once you've come out freer and full of deeper joy, you're willing to experience whatever is needed in order to know Him better.

Use your circumstances to strengthen those around you. Talk about the hard parts and the beauty that comes from ashes. Ask God to show you what He is doing in your life and how you can best share that with others.

Sometimes the best moment to sing a victory song is
in the middle of your battle.
JEREMY RIDDLE, WORSHIP LEADER

GOD'S PROMISES
ABOUT ADVERSITY

*I called to the L*ORD *in my distress; I called to my God.*
From His temple He heard my voice.
II SAMUEL 22:7 HCSB

God blesses those who patiently endure testing and
temptation. Afterward they will receive the crown of
life that God has promised to those who love Him.
JAMES 1:12 NLT

He heals the brokenhearted
and binds up their wounds.
PSALM 147:3 NKJV

God, my shepherd! I don't need a thing.
PSALM 23:1 THE MESSAGE

We are pressed on every side by troubles, but not
crushed and broken. We are perplexed because we
don't know why things happen as they do,
but we don't give up and quit.
II CORINTHIANS 4:8 TLB

6

ANXIETY AND
WORRY

Don't be anxious about tomorrow.
God will take care of your tomorrow too.
MATTHEW 6:34 TLB

Isn't it just like us to assume that God isn't paying attention? We aren't comfortable or we feel insecure, so we assume that God isn't holding up His end of the bargain.

But what if He is the perfect example of how we should carry ourselves through the storm? What if, instead of assuming He's got it wrong, we trust that He's got it very right? What if our default is to look to Him and mimic His movements? Chances are, we would experience a much more peaceful existence. And instead of being shaken by whatever comes our way, we would likely be the ones doing the shaking.

When we choose thankful prayer over wallowing
in anxiety and worry, we are demonstrating an
unwavering trust in God.
PRISCILLA SHIRER, AUTHOR

GOD'S PROMISES ABOUT ANXIETY AND WORRY

Let Him have all your worries and cares,
for He is always thinking about you
and watching everything that concerns you.
I PETER 5:7 TLB

Don't worry about anything; instead, pray about
everything; tell God your needs, and don't forget
to thank Him for His answers.
PHILIPPIANS 4:6 TLB

There is far more to your inner life than the food you
put in your stomach, more to your outer appearance
than the clothes you hang on your body.
Look at the ravens, free and unfettered, not tied down
to a job description, carefree in the care of God.
And you count far more.
LUKE 12:23–24 THE MESSAGE

Don't let this throw you. You trust God, don't you?
Trust Me.
JOHN 14:1 THE MESSAGE

Cast your burden on the LORD, and He will sustain
you; He will never allow the righteous to be shaken.
PSALM 55:22 HCSB

7

ASKING GOD

I tell you the truth, you will ask the Father directly,
and He will grant your request
because you use My name.
JOHN 16:23 NLT

So what's the trick to getting what we want from God? A trick question, right? Well...sort of! God gives according to His will. He knows that His will is best for us, and we don't always see the bigger picture.

But as we draw closer to Him and allow the Holy Spirit to do His transforming work in us, then little by little our hearts change. Our desires begin to line up with His desires. And in that way, we ask what He wants of us, and He delivers.

So the question isn't about how to manipulate God. It's about how we can line ourselves up with His will and then see blessing after blessing unfold.

When we need, God knows. When we ask, God listens.
When we believe, God works.
ANONYMOUS

GOD'S PROMISES
ABOUT ASKING HIM

You can get anything—
anything *you ask for in prayer—if you believe.*
MATTHEW 21:22 TLB

Don't bargain with God. Be direct.
Ask for what you need. This isn't a cat-and-mouse,
hide-and-seek game we're in.
MATTHEW 7:7–8 The Message

The urgent request of a righteous person
is very powerful in its effect.
JAMES 5:16 HCSB

Your Father knows exactly what you need even before
you ask Him!
MATTHEW 6:8 NLT

You didn't choose Me, remember; I chose you, and put
you in the world to bear fruit, fruit that won't spoil.
As fruit bearers, whatever you ask the Father in
relation to Me, He gives you.
JOHN 15:16 The Message

8

ATTITUDE

*You must have the same attitude
that Christ Jesus had.*
PHILIPPIANS 2:5 NLT

Choosing your attitude is as deliberate as choosing your outfit. How are you going to go about your day? Will you put on a veil of pessimism or entitlement? Or will you choose to wear kindness and encouragement? Will you hope for the best or expect the worst?

Just as it takes deliberate effort to put on pants and a shirt, it takes effort to wear the virtues given us by God—especially in the face of challenges. But consider it an honor. Like wearing a uniform to a job you love, it's a privilege to have His grace and mercy at our fingertips.

*Being negative only makes a difficult journey more
difficult. You may be given a cactus, but you don't
have to sit on it.*
JOYCE MEYER, AUTHOR

GOD'S PROMISES
ABOUT ATTITUDE

Rejoice in every day of life.
ECCLESIASTES 11:8 NLT

Finally, brothers, rejoice. Become mature, be encouraged, be of the same mind, be at peace, and the God of love and peace will be with you.
II CORINTHIANS 13:11 HCSB

Be glad and rejoice,
because your reward is great in heaven.
MATTHEW 5:12 HCSB

This is the day the Lord has made;
let us rejoice and be glad in it.
PSALM 118:24 HCSB

Rejoice always; pray without ceasing.
I THESSALONIANS 5:16–17 NASB

9

BEGINNING

Then God looked over all He had made,
and He saw that it was very good!
GENESIS 1:31 NLT

Getting a new job or position is the beginning of a chapter. It can be seen as the title page in a book: *Sarah Begins Work at Home Products, Inc.* But the bulk of the chapter—the story itself—gets written over time, as you immerse yourself in the company and the work. There will be high and low points, and all of it will lead to...yes, the next chapter title and the next part of the story.

The Lord often delivers us to the threshold of a new season. We may be given new opportunities. Or we may experience a new healing or deliverance. But the way those things play out in our lives takes time and partnership with the Holy Spirit.

There are far better things ahead
than any we leave behind.
C. S. LEWIS, THEOLOGIAN

GOD'S PROMISES
ABOUT BEGINNING

But forget all that—it is nothing compared to what I
am going to do. For I am about to do something new.
ISAIAH 43:18–19 NLT

You are being renewed in the spirit of your minds; you
put on the new self, the one created according to God's
likeness in righteousness and purity of the truth.
EPHESIANS 4:23–24 HCSB

There is one thing I always do.
Forgetting the past and straining toward what is
ahead, I keep trying to reach the goal and get the prize
for which God called me through Christ.
PHILIPPIANS 3:13–14 NCV

Then the One seated on the throne said,
"Look! I am making everything new."
REVELATION 21:5 HCSB

Do not despise these small beginnings,
for the LORD rejoices to see the work begin.
ZECHARIAH 4:10 NLT

10

BEHAVIOR

*Walk in a manner worthy of the God who calls you
into His own kingdom and glory.*
1 THESSALONIANS 2:12 NASB

You're contagious! Did you know? But in the very best way.

Every time you encourage someone...every time you let someone cut in line in front of you...every time you make a decision based on whatever is true, right, noble, lovely, pure, excellent, or praiseworthy (Phil. 4:8)...the goodness of God is poured out.

Of course, it works the other way too. Negative words and actions can also have an effect on those around us. It can be a challenge to live out the love of Jesus when circumstances are testing our emotions and patience. But every time we choose love, everyone wins.

*The challenge is not merely to do what God says
because He is God, but to desire what God says because
He is good.*
JOHN PIPER, AUTHOR

GOD'S PROMISES
ABOUT BEHAVIOR

*Here's how we can be sure that we know God in the
right way: Keep His commandments.*
I JOHN 2:3 The Message

*Oh, the joys of those who do not follow the advice of
the wicked, or stand around with sinners, or join in
with mockers. But they delight in the law of the LORD,
meditating on it day and night.*
PSALM 1:1–2 NLT

*Pray this way for kings and all who are in authority
so that we can live peaceful and quiet lives
marked by godliness and dignity.*
I TIMOTHY 2:2 NLT

*But prove yourselves doers of the word,
and not merely hearers who delude themselves.*
JAMES 1:22 NASB

*Be an example to them by doing good works
of every kind.*
TITUS 2:7 NLT

11

BELIEFS

I have come as a light into the world, that whoever believes in Me should not abide in darkness.
JOHN 12:46 NKJV

You might be the first in your family who is a believer or just the next in line. You might be the one hoping that your sister or friend or uncle or grandfather will one day choose Jesus. In any case, we know that belief in Him always carries an impact to those around us. He is the Sower of very good seeds, and your life is like a spreader. Stay connected to Him and those seeds will go out wherever you walk and live.

It's up to Him to water those seeds. He might use you or other people you don't even know. The Holy Spirit will always stir up the soil of faith when the time is right.

God is who He says He is. God can do what He says He can do. I am who God says I am. I can do all things through Christ. God's Word is alive and active in me.
BETH MOORE, EVANGELIST

GOD'S PROMISES
ABOUT BELIEFS

Jesus said, "Because you have seen Me, you have
believed. Those who believe without seeing are blessed."
JOHN 20:29 HCSB

I tell you the truth, whoever believes in Me
will do the same things that I do. Those who believe
will do even greater things than these,
because I am going to the Father.
JOHN 14:12 NCV

All things are possible for the one who believes.
MARK 9:23 NCV

I know the One I have believed in and am persuaded
that He is able to guard what has been
entrusted to me until that day.
II TIMOTHY 1:12 HCSB

Choose today whom you will serve.... As for me and
my family, we will serve the LORD.
JOSHUA 24:15 NLT

12

CHARACTER, HONESTY, AND INTEGRITY

Guard your heart above all else,
for it determines the course of your life.
PROVERBS 4:23 NLT

Your friend shows up to lunch after a vacation overseas. You notice she has a fancy new handbag. "I got it at a market there for such an incredible price—only twenty dollars! It would cost two hundred here!" As you admire the bag, you glance at the familiar logo of the name brand. You squint...and see that the famous label is misspelled. You've spotted an impostor.

The true things of God don't have to try to convince anyone of their goodness. The closer you scrutinize, the more integrity you see in His handiwork. Not so with impostors, who have to hide blemishes. The Lord doesn't mind close examination. In fact, He welcomes it.

Integrity, the choice between what's convenient
and what's right.
TONY DUNGY, FOOTBALL COACH

GOD'S PROMISES ABOUT CHARACTER, HONESTY, AND INTEGRITY

Work hard to prove that you really are among those God has called and chosen. Do these things, and you will never fall away.
II PETER 1:10 NLT

Honesty lives confident and carefree, but Shifty is sure to be exposed.
PROVERBS 10:9 THE MESSAGE

Let integrity and uprightness preserve me, for I wait for You.
PSALM 25:21 NKJV

The godly are directed by honesty.
PROVERBS 11:5 NLT

He stores up success for the upright; He is a shield for those who live with integrity.
PROVERBS 2:7 HCSB

13

CHRIST'S LOVE

I am the good shepherd.
The good shepherd lays down His life for the sheep.
JOHN 10:11 HCSB

*W*hen in doubt, love it out. That was her motto as she worked as a counselor at the children's camp for cancer patients. Those kids were often so starved for love and attention. Their bodies, families, and lives had been through so much. They just needed love.

Sometimes she wondered if she cared too much. Was that even possible, to over-love? Could she give those children too much kindness and energy?

One day she confided in a friend. "Well," the friend responded, "answer me this. Can you imagine reaching heaven and having Jesus tell you that you loved too much? Or might it be more likely that He would say you loved too little? Which would you want to hear?"

From that point she knew. Love is an endless commodity that is worth giving and giving away.

Find the things that stir your affections for Christ and saturate your life in them. Find the things that rob you of that affection and walk away from them. That's the Christian life as easy as I can explain it for you.

MATT CHANDLER, PASTOR

GOD'S PROMISES ABOUT CHRIST'S LOVE

Let your roots grow down into Him,
and let your lives be built on Him. Then your faith
will grow strong in the truth you were taught,
and you will overflow with thankfulness.
COLOSSIANS 2:7 NLT

I've loved you the way My Father has loved Me.
Make yourselves at home in My love.
JOHN 15:9 THE MESSAGE

No one has greater love than this,
that someone would lay down his life for his friends.
JOHN 15:13 HCSB

That's what Christ did definitively: suffered because
of others' sins, the Righteous One for the unrighteous
ones. He went through it all—was put to death
and then made alive—to bring us to God.
I PETER 3:18 THE MESSAGE

For this is how God loved the world: He gave His one
and only Son, so that everyone who believes in Him
will not perish but have eternal life.
JOHN 3:16 NLT

14

CIRCUMSTANCES

Think it over. God will make it all plain.
II TIMOTHY 2:7 THE MESSAGE

If you ask someone what skydiving is like, they might say exhilarating or terrifying or like jumping out of a flying airplane! But until you strap yourself into that harness...until you listen to the training, sign a waiver saying you know you could die, take off, wait for the count, and then push off the edge into earsplitting winds as you plummet to the earth...you can't ever really know what skydiving is like.

God's answers often come through experience. Because by knowing instead of just hearing, we get all the feelings and understanding that can come no other way. God's character is revealed in experience. And we gain compassion for others when we've been there ourselves.

Embrace uncertainty.
Some of the most beautiful chapters in our lives
won't have a title until much later.
BOB GOFF, AUTHOR

GOD'S PROMISES
ABOUT CIRCUMSTANCES

When you go through deep waters,
I will be with you. When you go through rivers
of difficulty, you will not drown. When you walk
through the fire of oppression, you will not be burned
up; the flames will not consume you.
ISAIAH 43:2 NLT

The LORD will be a refuge for His people,
a strong fortress.
JOEL 3:16 NLT

The LORD is a refuge for the oppressed,
a refuge in times of trouble.
PSALM 9:9 HCSB

Cast your burden on the LORD, and He shall sustain
you; He shall never permit the righteous to be moved.
PSALM 55:22 NKJV

I have learned in whatever state I am, to be content.
PHILIPPIANS 4:11 NKJV

15

COMFORTING OTHERS

Carry one another's burdens;
in this way you will fulfill the law of Christ.
GALATIANS 6:2 HCSB

She had just flown to Denver a month before, to take care of a sick friend. And then she received the sad news: her friend's dad had passed away. So without a blink, she turned right around and bought a plane ticket to Denver. Again. To offer nothing more than the ministry of presence.

This ministry requires no special training. It simply requires a person to...well, be present. To show up. It's the kind of love that says, "Whatever you need, I'm here for you."

God says to us, "I will draw near to you" (see James 4:8). "Never will I leave you" (Hebrews 13:5). When we show people the kind of nearness love, we're showing them the true heart of God.

There are two types of people:
those who walk into a room and say,
"Well, here I am!" and those who come in
and say, "Ah, there you are."
FREDERICK L. COLLINS, AUTHOR

GOD'S PROMISES ABOUT COMFORTING OTHERS

So encourage each other and give each other strength,
just as you are doing now.
I THESSALONIANS 5:11 NCV

Never walk away from someone who deserves help;
your hand is God's hand for that person.
PROVERBS 3:27 THE MESSAGE

Just as you want others to do for you,
do the same for them.
LUKE 6:31 HCSB

Christ encourages you,
and His love comforts you. God's Spirit unites you,
and you are concerned for others.
PHILIPPIANS 2:1 CEV

He comforts us in all our affliction,
so that we may be able to comfort those
who are in any kind of affliction,
through the comfort we ourselves receive from God.
II CORINTHIANS 1:4 HCSB

16

COMMUNICATION

*A word fitly spoken is like apples of gold
in settings of silver.*
PROVERBS 25:11 NKJV

"But why didn't you come to me?" A long string of gossip had led to the widespread belief that John was going to fire multiple people within the week. As soon as he heard about it, John went to the source. The frustrated employee finally explained that she'd messed up on a project and expected John to be mad. So she lashed out behind his back instead of talking with him. "I just didn't know how to talk to you about it."

Prayer only works when we go to Him. The same rules apply as with people: be honest, listen well, and have a humble heart. The Holy Spirit is there for the express purpose of mediating the conversation.

*When we can talk about our feelings, they become
less overwhelming, less upsetting, and less scary. The
people we trust with that important talk can help us
know that we are not alone.*
FRED ROGERS, TELEVISION PERSONALITY

GOD'S PROMISES
ABOUT COMMUNICATION

But encourage each other daily,
while it is still called today, so that none of you
is hardened by sin's deception.
HEBREWS 3:13 HCSB

What you have said in the dark will be heard in the
light, and what you have whispered in an inner room
will be shouted from the housetops.
LUKE 12:3 NCV

If you claim to be religious
but don't control your tongue,
you are fooling yourself,
and your religion is worthless.
JAMES 1:26 NLT

Pleasant words are a honeycomb:
sweet to the taste and health to the body.
PROVERBS 16:24 HCSB

They make a lot of sense, these wise folks; whenever
they speak, their reputation increases.
PROVERBS 16:23 THE MESSAGE

17

CONFIDENCE

*Let us go right in to God Himself, with true hearts
fully trusting Him to receive us.*
HEBREWS 10:22 TLB

The stars in the sky can be billions of light-years away. Yet their shining is so pure that it can be seen by the human eye. Other debris, asteroids, and satellites float around in space, but we cannot see them. It takes the purest light to shine the brightest. What debris or dark matter interferes with the light you carry? Ask the Lord to remove it.

And at the same time, be encouraged that the light of Jesus can shine through the dark, even where imperfections exist. You are the perfect vessel for His work, and you can be confident that you make a bright difference in the world around you. So go on out there and shine!

*You can't lose confidence in yourself, or you've lost
already. When you get knocked down, you've got to
keep getting back up.*
TIM TEBOW, ATHLETE

GOD'S PROMISES
ABOUT CONFIDENCE

*Dear friends, if we don't feel guilty, we can come to
God with bold confidence. And we will receive from
Him whatever we ask because we obey Him and do the
things that please Him.*
I JOHN 3:21-22 NLT

*Therefore, we may boldly say: The Lord is my helper;
I will not be afraid. What can man do to me?*
HEBREWS 13:6 HCSB

*Here on earth you will have many trials and sorrows.
But take heart, because I have overcome the world.*
JOHN 16:33 NLT

*Be strong and courageous, and do the work. Don't be
afraid or discouraged, for the LORD God, my God, is
with you. He won't leave you or forsake you.*
I CHRONICLES 28:20 HCSB

*I lift my eyes toward the mountains. Where will my
help come from? My help comes from the LORD, the
Maker of heaven and earth.*
PSALM 121:1-2 HCSB

18

CONSCIENCE

*Create in me a clean heart, O God. Renew a loyal
spirit within me.*
PSALM 51:10 NLT

Is our love supply bottomless or boxed in? Imagine a woman examining her cupboard when her neighbor asks for a cup of sugar. "I have about two cups left. I might want it later, so I can give you just a tablespoon now." The neighbor will remember this moment. And if the woman needs two eggs for a recipe later, the neighbor may respond, "I have four eggs and may be extra hungry tomorrow morning. So I can give you just one egg now."

Our heart status matters more than our pocket status. Are we acting out of love or with respect to what we think we can spare? Whatever our hearts pour out is how much room we have to receive.

*There comes a time when one must take a position
that is neither safe nor political nor popular, but he
must take it because conscience tells him it is right.*
MARTIN LUTHER KING JR., MINISTER

GOD'S PROMISES
ABOUT CONSCIENCE

*Dear friend, guard Clear Thinking and Common
Sense with your life; don't for a minute lose sight of
them.... You'll travel safely, you'll neither tire nor trip.*
PROVERBS 3:21, 23 THE MESSAGE

*Now the goal of our instruction is love that comes from
a pure heart, a good conscience, and a sincere faith.*
I TIMOTHY 1:5 HCSB

*Because of this, I always try to maintain a clear
conscience before God and all people.*
ACTS 24:16 NLT

*Let us come near to God with a sincere heart and a
sure faith, because we have been made free from a
guilty conscience, and our bodies have been washed
with pure water.*
HEBREWS 10:22 NCV

Indeed, the kingdom of God is within you.
LUKE 17:21 NKJV

19

CONTENTMENT

*But godliness with contentment
is a great gain.*
I TIMOTHY 6:6 HCSB

You, friend, are a smart person. You know many things. You've been given all sorts of knowledge and experience. But even the wisest and oldest among us is a mere blip on the screen of God's eternal plan. He is the Master Architect, with a view to everything. Before time began. For the last 2000+ years. And until a new heaven and a new earth take place.

Don't be offended or hurt if something doesn't make sense. There's *a lot* you don't know, along with everyone else! God is working all things together for good...and that takes a lot of orchestration. Simply trusting Him and following His lead are the most peaceful, restful ways to go.

*Walk with the Lord,
and you'll always be going in the right direction.*
ROY LESSIN, AUTHOR

GOD'S PROMISES
ABOUT CONTENTMENT

I will praise the Lord no matter what happens.
PSALM 34:1 TLB

The Lord will guide you continually,
and satisfy you with all good things.
ISAIAH 58:11 TLB

I have learned in whatever state I am,
to be content.
PHILIPPIANS 4:11 NKJV

Make sure that your character is free from the love of
money, being content with what you have;
for He Himself has said, "I WILL NEVER DESERT you,
NOR WILL I EVER FORSAKE you."
HEBREWS 13:5 NASB

You will experience God's peace, which exceeds
anything we can understand. His peace will guard
your hearts and minds as you live in Christ Jesus.
PHILIPPIANS 4:7 NLT

20

COURAGE

Be strong! Be courageous! Do not be afraid...for the
Lord your God will be with you.
DEUTERONOMY 31:6 TLB

Each day is a chance to step out in boldness. That doesn't mean pride or false courage. It takes a very humble heart and a very keen sense of awareness of our less-than abilities apart from Christ. But every day, there's a bucket of new mercies ready to shower down on you. There's a shiny suit of armor waiting to wrap you in readiness. Whatever happened yesterday—and whatever will happen tomorrow—have no part in who you choose to be today. In whose you choose you remember you are.

You belong to the Lord. No self-consciousness or timidity will change that. The very best vessels for His kingdom are those who say, "Okay, God...let's go after it! Use me however You want."

Courage is found in unlikely places.
J. R. R. TOLKIEN, AUTHOR

GOD'S PROMISES ABOUT COURAGE

Be on guard. Stand firm in the faith.
Be courageous. Be strong.
I CORINTHIANS 16:13 NLT

For God has not given us a spirit of fearfulness, but
one of power, love, and sound judgment.
II TIMOTHY 1:7 HCSB

I can do all things through Him who strengthens me.
PHILIPPIANS 4:13 NASB

But He said to them, "It is I; do not be afraid."
JOHN 6:20 NKJV

Yes, indeed—God is my salvation.
I trust, I won't be afraid. God—yes GOD!—
is my strength and song,
best of all, my salvation!
ISAIAH 12:2 THE MESSAGE

21

CRITICISM

LORD, set up a guard for my mouth;
keep watch at the door of my lips.
PSALM 141:3 HCSB

There's nothing quite like being rejected. It's hard! We are made for connection and community, so the mere idea of a broken connection goes against our grain.

But we know that life has hard things. Jesus promised, in fact (John 16:33). We can count on difficulties coming our way, and it's no surprise to Him.

Jesus has been there. He knows rejection on a deeper level and in more brutal ways than we will ever experience in our lifetime. But He also received the King's reward in the end.

We can stay strong when we are criticized or rejected. We can keep our eyes on Jesus, cry out to Him, and remember that everything turns out victorious in the end.

We have a tendency to want the other person
to be a finished product, while we give ourselves
the grace to evolve.
BISHOP T. D. JAKES

GOD'S PROMISES
ABOUT CRITICISM

Do not judge others, and you will not be judged.
Do not condemn others, or it will all come back
against you. Forgive others, and you will be forgiven.
LUKE 6:37 NLT

It is foolish to belittle one's neighbor;
a sensible person keeps quiet.
PROVERBS 11:12 NLT

Do everything without grumbling and arguing,
so that you may be blameless and pure,
children of God who are faultless
in a crooked and perverted generation,
among whom you shine like stars in the world.
PHILIPPIANS 2:14–15 HCSB

Those who control their tongue will have a long life;
opening your mouth can ruin everything.
PROVERBS 13:3 NLT

These are the words in my mouth;
these are what I chew on and pray.
Accept them when I place them on the morning altar,
O God, my Altar-Rock, God, Priest-of-My-Altar.
PSALM 19:14 THE MESSAGE

22

DECISIONS

But if any of you needs wisdom,
you should ask God for it.
He is generous to everyone and
will give you wisdom without criticizing you.
JAMES 1:5 NCV

Behold: the cereal aisle. Fifty glorious feet of every color, shape, and flavor of sugary goodness. Or if you prefer: gluten-free grains, sugarless oats, and athlete-approved flakes for all. If you can imagine a box made for milk and mornings, it probably exists at a store in your city.

We love choices! And if we don't see what we want, we make our own! Although cereal hasn't been around since the beginning, the desire for independence has. People have searched for answers other than God. But there is only One. No other god can hold a candle to the Alpha and Omega. Some decisions we make are harmless. But sometimes the very best choice is the only One that makes sense.

You need to make the right decision—firmly and
decisively—and then stick with it, with God's help.
BILLY GRAHAM

GOD'S PROMISES
ABOUT DECISIONS

In every way be an example of doing good deeds.
When you teach, do it with honesty and seriousness.
TITUS 2:7 NCV

We can make our own plans, but the LORD gives the
right answer. People may be pure in their own eyes,
but the LORD examines their motives.
PROVERBS 16:1-2 NLT

Blessed is the man who walks not in the counsel of the
ungodly, nor stands in the path of sinners, nor sits in
the seat of the scornful;
PSALM 1:1 NKJV

The highway of the upright avoids evil; the one who
guards his way protects his life.
PROVERBS 16:17 HCSB

23

DISAPPOINTMENTS

He heals the brokenhearted
and binds up their wounds.
PSALM 147:3 HCSB

Nothing happens apart from God's knowledge. Just take a minute to think about what it would be like to have a God who could be surprised by circumstances, and you'll see how silly that sounds! "What??" He might say. "Wait, I didn't know Peyton was going through such a thing. Who let that happen? Why wasn't I informed? Oh dear. What am I going to do now??"

Hopefully that sounds ridiculous to you! Because even though hard or painful things happen, Romans 8:28 promises that God can work out every single detail for good to those who love Him. It just takes leaning in, asking tough questions, and believing with your whole heart.

God is good. He knows what He is doing.
When you can't trace His hand, trust His heart.
MAX LUCADO, PASTOR

GOD'S PROMISES
ABOUT DISAPPOINTMENTS

*Then they cried out to the LORD in their trouble,
and He delivered them out of their distresses.*
PSALM 107:6 NKJV

*He will not be afraid of evil tidings; His heart is
steadfast, trusting in the LORD.*
PSALM 112:7 NKJV

*Many adversities come to the one who is righteous, but
the LORD delivers him from them all.*
PSALM 34:19 HCSB

*And you have forgotten the exhortation which
speaks to you as to sons: "My son, do not despise the
chastening of the LORD, nor be discouraged when you
are rebuked by Him."*
HEBREWS 12:5 NKJV

*Those who cry as they plant crops
will sing at harvest time.*
PSALM 126:5 NCV

24

DISCIPLINE

To learn, you must love discipline;
it is stupid to hate correction.
PROVERBS 12:1 NLT

There's always a reason for God's discipline. His justice, even toward your character, is worth the temporary discomfort. The wise person who experiences His discipline will lean in even closer to hear Him. "I don't want to go through this again, so teach me all You have for me to learn this time around. Thank You for loving me so much to show me the way."

The unwise person, on the other hand, looks for excuses and escapes. She will most likely end up "learning" the same lesson over and over again.

Discipline lasts for a short season; shorter if you're a fast learner. The freedom and joy of eternity will last forever.

The notion of freedom proclaimed by the modern
world is anti-discipline. But true freedom cannot be
separated from discipline.
MATTHEW KELLY, MOTIVATIONAL SPEAKER

GOD'S PROMISES
ABOUT DISCIPLINE

Hold tight to good advice; don't relax your grip.
Guard it well—your life is at stake!
PROVERBS 4:13 THE MESSAGE

Work willingly at whatever you do, as though you
were working for the Lord rather than for people.
COLOSSIANS 3:23 NLT

But the fruit of the Spirit is love, joy, peace, patience,
kindness, goodness, faith, gentleness, self-control.
Against such things there is no law.
GALATIANS 5:22–23 HCSB

Finishing is better than starting.
Patience is better than pride.
ECCLESIASTES 7:8 NLT

A final word: Be strong in the Lord
and in His mighty power.
EPHESIANS 6:10 NLT

25

DREAMS

When dreams come true at last, there is life and joy.
PROVERBS 13:12 TLB

Before a child learns to temper her imagination, she can think up impossible storylines with the least likely adventures, and the most amazing gusto. Where else are you likely to hear of the purple penguin who befriends a spotted buffalo as they search for rainbow tokens worth special candy prizes in the lightning-bug forest?

But even as wild as a child's imagination can be, the plans of God are more unfathomable. We see dim glimpses through the Word: seas of glass, streets of gold, angels like many-eyed beings...but God's dreams and plans for us will never be seen this side of heaven. So for now, dream huge. Keep dreaming. And watch as He overwhelms you with even more.

But the greatest dream of all is to know God and to know what He has intended for your life.
RAVI ZACHARIAS, AUTHOR

GOD'S PROMISES
ABOUT DREAMS

*He gives those who respect Him what they want. He
listens when they cry, and He saves them.*
PSALM 145:19 NCV

*Don't waste time arguing over foolish ideas and silly
myths and legends. Spend your time and energy in the
exercise of keeping spiritually fit.*
I TIMOTHY 4:7 TLB

Where there is no vision, the people perish.
PROVERBS 29:18 KJV

*But we are hoping for something we do not have yet,
and are waiting for it patiently.*
ROMANS 8:25 NCV

*Now may the God of hope fill you with all joy and
peace as you believe in Him so that you may overflow
with hope by the power of the Holy Spirit.*
ROMANS 15:13 HCSB

26

ENCOURAGEMENT

So encourage each other and give each other strength,
just as you are doing now.
I THESSALONIANS 5:11 NCV

Sometimes it's so helpful to hear, "You're doing a good job!" A mom of teens needs to hear that often. A husband needs to know he's a good provider and protector. A pastor needs to be reminded that his care and commitment are serving the kingdom beautifully.

There are many more people along a marathon route than just the runners. Spectators hold signs and cowbells, yelling encouragement. At stations for water, the "Keep going; you're doing great!" messages from the volunteers make a big difference.

Let's face it—life's tough! We can wonder if we're really making a mark for good. Learn from the apostle Paul, who took time to write "Keep on doing what you're doing," and go encourage someone today.

In calling, in purpose, in giving, in grace, no one can
ever take your place. With words to encourage and
arms to embrace, no one can ever take your place.
Through heart, hands, touch, and face,
no one can ever take your place.
ROY LESSIN, AUTHOR

GOD'S PROMISES
ABOUT ENCOURAGEMENT

So then, let us aim for harmony in the church
and try to build each other up.
ROMANS 14:19 NLT

Bear one another's burdens,
and so fulfill the law of Christ.
GALATIANS 6:2 NKJV

When you talk, do not say harmful things,
but say what people need—words that will help others
become stronger. Then what you say will do good
to those who listen to you.
EPHESIANS 4:29 NCV

Warn the freeloaders to get a move on.
Gently encourage the stragglers, and reach out
for the exhausted, pulling them to their feet. Be patient
with each person, attentive to individual needs.
I THESSALONIANS 5:14 The Message

27

ENTHUSIASM

Whatever you do, do it enthusiastically,
as something done for the Lord and not for men.
COLOSSIANS 3:23 HCSB

What wouldn't a die-hard fan do to sit on the 50-yard line during the Super Bowl? How many chores and how much homework would a young girl do to be allowed to see that one band in concert?

Perhaps "fandom" of this world is put into place so that we can experience the true level of what passion for the Lord could look like. Telling everyone what you get to do! Losing your voice for the excitement and screaming! Talking for hours on end to fellow fans!

Of course, head-over-heels love for Jesus looks a bit different because motivations are different. But maybe we can use outside examples to examine our own hearts about our enthusiasm for Christ.

Wherever you are, be all there. Live to the hilt every
situation you believe to be the will of God.
JIM ELLIOT, MISSIONARY

GOD'S PROMISES
ABOUT ENTHUSIASM

Do your work with enthusiasm.
Work as if you were serving the Lord,
not as if you were serving only men and women.
EPHESIANS 6:7 NCV

A glad heart makes a happy face;
a broken heart crushes the spirit.
PROVERBS 15:13 NLT

I will keep on expecting You to help me.
I praise You more and more.
PSALM 71:14 TLB

Rejoice always!
Pray constantly.
Give thanks in everything,
for this is God's will for you in Christ Jesus.
I THESSALONIANS 5:16–18 HCSB

Revel in His holy Name, GOD-seekers,
be jubilant! Study GOD and His strength,
seek His presence day and night.
I CHRONICLES 16:10–11 THE MESSAGE

28

FAILURE

The godly may trip seven times,
but they will get up again.
PROVERBS 24:16 NLT

You've probably heard a phrase similar to this: the road to destruction is paved with good intentions. In other words, it's very easy to imagine doing a good thing and quite another to actually follow through.

We are human, after all. Imperfect, messy, gloriously beautiful humans who need the grace of God. We also sometimes need to be reminded of why we need Him.

Don't be discouraged if you fail, even if you meant well. Instead, that's a great opportunity to remember your humanness and thank the Lord for His mercy. Ask for His forgiveness. Then get up and try again. He is, after all, the God of second chances.

There are no super saints...
only people who don't quit.
MISTY EDWARDS, WORSHIP LEADER

GOD'S PROMISES
ABOUT FAILURE

The LORD is near to those who have a broken heart.
PSALM 34:18 NKJV

If you listen to correction to improve your life,
you will live among the wise.
PROVERBS 15:31 NCV

We are hard-pressed on every side, yet not crushed;
we are perplexed, but not in despair.
II CORINTHIANS 4:8 NKJV

But as for you, be strong;
don't be discouraged, for your work has a reward.
II CHRONICLES 15:7 HCSB

Weeping may endure for a night,
but joy comes in the morning.
PSALM 30:5 NKJV

29

FAITH

Don't be afraid. Only believe.
MARK 5:36 HCSB

The very definition of faith includes the requirement that you not be able to see into the future. If you could, then it wouldn't be faith—which is "the substance of things hoped for; the evidence of things not seen" (Hebrews 11:1 KJV). Faith means trusting God for the path ahead; trusting that He is good and knows better than we do.

Another element of faith is to not worry, which is an attempt to control the uncontrollable. Our most important job, in times of the unknown, is to keep our eyes on Jesus and follow His lead.

Faith is acting like God is telling the truth.
PRISCILLA SHIRER, AUTHOR

GOD'S PROMISES
ABOUT FAITH

But let us who live in the light be clearheaded,
protected by the armor of faith and love, and wearing
as our helmet the confidence of our salvation.
I THESSALONIANS 5:8 NLT

What is faith? It is the confident assurance that
something we want is going to happen.
HEBREWS 11:1 TLB

For truly I say to you, if you have faith the size of a
mustard seed, you will say to this mountain, "Move
from here to there," and it will move; and nothing will
be impossible to you.
MATTHEW 17:20 NASB

Don't be afraid, because I am your God. I will make
you strong and will help you; I will support you with
My right hand that saves you.
ISAIAH 41:10 NCV

Blessed are those who have not seen
and yet have believed.
JOHN 20:29 NKJV

30

FEAR

The LORD is my light and my salvation—
whom should I fear?
The LORD is the stronghold of my life—
of whom should I be afraid?
PSALM 27:1 HCSB

Two sisters were taken to Disneyland by their parents. The older girl worried about the rides. Would she get sick? She worried about being away from home. Would the dog miss them too much? Would the airplane ride be scary?

The younger girl imagined that the trip would be wonderful. She thought of the characters, balloons, treats, and fun rides. She thought of the stories she'd have to tell when she got back. Mostly she thought about the unknown possibilities.

Who do you think had more fun? Fear is a life-stealer, a thief of fun. God suggests we not worry or be afraid, because there's no good that comes from it. All the good comes from living expectantly for our amazing God to be His amazing self.

Fear doesn't shut you down; it wakes you up.
VERONICA ROTH, NOVELIST

GOD'S PROMISES
ABOUT FEAR

If you will stir up this inner power,
you will never be afraid.
II TIMOTHY 1:8 TLB

Peace I leave with you; My peace I give to you;
not as the world gives do I give to you. Do not let
your heart be troubled, nor let it be fearful.
JOHN 14:27 NASB

But He said to them, "It is I; do not be afraid."
JOHN 6:20 NKJV

Fear not, for I am with you; be not dismayed, for I am
your God. I will strengthen you, yes, I will help you,
I will uphold you with My righteous right hand.
ISAIAH 41:10 NKJV

Even when I walk through the darkest valley, I will
not be afraid, for You are close beside me. Your rod
and Your staff protect and comfort me.
PSALM 23:4 NLT

31

FEARING GOD

Fear of the LORD is the foundation of true knowledge,
but fools despise wisdom and discipline.
PROVERBS 1:7 NLT

You may have seen videos on the internet where people cause explosions due to careless fireworks. You've probably heard stories of divers swimming with sharks who wished they hadn't. People get braver and braver with dangerous things if they haven't experienced the danger firsthand.

A healthy respect is important to have when you're in the presence of any sort of power. And of course, the Lord is the most supreme Source of power there is. Fearing God is not a matter of being afraid of Him. It's a matter of standing in great awe, understanding that He is far beyond comprehension and recognizing that He and His power cannot be harnessed.

Stand in awe of God and you will be walking in the most rudimentary form of wisdom.

Obedience is the outward evidence
of the true fear of the Lord.
JOHN BEVERE, AUTHOR

GOD'S PROMISES ABOUT FEARING HIM

The lovingkindness of the LORD is from everlasting to everlasting on those who fear Him, and His righteousness to children's children, to those who keep His covenant and remember His precepts to do them.
PSALM 103:17–18 NASB

Fear the LORD, you His godly people, for those who fear Him will have all they need.
PSALM 34:9 NLT

Those who respect the LORD will live and be satisfied, unbothered by trouble.
PROVERBS 19:23 NCV

But the eyes of the Lord are watching over those who fear Him, who rely upon His steady love. He will keep them from death even in times of famine!
PSALM 33:18 TLB

The life-giving Spirit of GOD will hover over him, the Spirit that brings wisdom and understanding, the Spirit that gives direction and builds strength, the Spirit that instills knowledge and Fear-of-GOD.
ISAIAH 11:2 THE MESSAGE

32

FOLLOWING CHRIST

*Then He said to the crowd, "If any of you wants to be
My follower, you must give up your own way,
take up your cross daily, and follow Me."*
LUKE 9:23 NLT

There are two ways to live in this world, at the risk of sounding like a Shakespeare play: to do, and to be. Fitting ourselves into culture, acting like everyone else, that is us doing the doing. But letting the Lord lead us through culture, loving everyone around us: that is Him doing the transforming.

It's a bit like driving a car vs. being a passenger. We can take the wheel and be responsible for all the road hazards and safe driving, or we can enjoy the scenery and go where He takes us.

Either way, things get done. The question is whose things, in what order, and according to which agenda. God's is always the best and most enjoyable!

*Following Christ isn't something that can be done
half-heartedly or on the side. It is not a label we
can display when it is useful. It must be central to
everything we do and are.*
FRANCIS CHAN, PASTOR

GOD'S PROMISES ABOUT FOLLOWING CHRIST

Put GOD in charge of your work,
then what you've planned will take place.
PROVERBS 16:3 THE MESSAGE

You go before me and follow me.
You place Your hand of blessing on my head.
PSALM 139:5 NLT

Behold, I stand at the door and knock. If anyone hears
My voice and opens the door, I will come in to him
and dine with him, and he with Me.
REVELATION 3:20 NKJV

But whoever keeps His word,
truly in him the love of God is perfected.
This is how we know we are in Him: the one who says
he remains in Him should walk just as He walked.
I JOHN 2:5-6 HCSB

Walk in a manner worthy of the God
who calls you into His own kingdom and glory.
I THESSALONIANS 2:12 NASB

33

FORGIVENESS

And be kind to one another, tenderhearted, forgiving
one another, even as God in Christ forgave you.
EPHESIANS 4:32 NKJV

Forgiveness is a gift first given to us by Jesus, and a gift we can give ourselves. Forgiving someone does not excuse bad behavior. It simply means that you release another person from owing you anything for their mistakes.

It has been said that not forgiving someone out of spite is like cutting yourself with a knife, trying to get another person to bleed. A graphic image. But it illustrates well that the only one unforgiveness truly hurts is the person who refuses to give it.

It can be so hard to forgive someone who has hurt us so badly. But offering forgiveness is truly life-changing.

Forgiveness is the key that unlocks the door of
resentment and the handcuffs of hate.
It is the power that breaks the chains
of bitterness and the shackles of selfishness.
CORRIE ten BOOM, SURVIVOR

GOD'S PROMISES
ABOUT FORGIVENESS

Judge not, and you shall not be judged.
Condemn not, and you shall not be condemned.
Forgive, and you will be forgiven.
LUKE 6:37 NKJV

But I say to you, love your enemies
and pray for those who persecute you.
MATTHEW 5:44 NASB

And when you assume the posture of prayer, remember
that it's not all asking. If you have anything against
someone, forgive—only then will your heavenly Father
be inclined to also wipe your slate clean of sins.
MARK 11:25 THE MESSAGE

God blesses those who are merciful,
for they will be shown mercy.
MATTHEW 5:7 NLT

34

FRIENDS AND FRIENDSHIP

*Oil and incense bring joy to the heart, and the
sweetness of a friend is better than self-counsel.*
PROVERBS 27:9 HCSB

At the school was a playground. On the playground was a bench. On the bench sat a boy. And the boy needed a friend. But this wasn't a sad story. Because this bench was a friend bench—a place for kids to go and wait if they wanted to play with someone at recess. And other kids knew to pay attention to the bench. If they saw someone sitting there, they would go and make a new friend.

So the boy didn't sit there for long before a kid from another class came over and introduced himself. And soon the boy was laughing in a rousing game of tag.

*You've got what it takes to be a great friend, just as
Jesus is. All you need to do is watch for the chance.
But life's joys are only joys if they can be shared.*
RAVI ZACHARIAS, AUTHOR

GOD'S PROMISES ABOUT FRIENDS AND FRIENDSHIP

How wonderful, how beautiful,
when brothers and sisters get along!
PSALM 133:1 THE MESSAGE

Two are better than one.
ECCLESIASTES 4:9 NKJV

Friends love through all kinds of weather, and
families stick together in all kinds of trouble.
PROVERBS 17:17 THE MESSAGE

As iron sharpens iron,
so people can improve each other.
PROVERBS 27:17 NCV

Bear with each other, and forgive each other.
If someone does wrong to you, forgive that person
because the Lord forgave you.
COLOSSIANS 3:13 NCV

35

GIFTS

Every desirable and beneficial gift comes out of heaven. The gifts are rivers of light cascading down from the Father of Light. There is nothing deceitful in God, nothing two-faced, nothing fickle.
JAMES 1:17 THE MESSAGE

Nothing from God is wasted. Absolutely nothing! That means that beyond our needs, which He always provides—God also supplies us with gifts, treasures, and resources to be put to good use. If He only gave you what you needed for survival, then what would you have to give away? Loving others is a necessary part of your life!

He knows what you need to sustain your life and stay healthy. He also knows that an overflow of favor, love, grace, and mercy works in everyone's favor. So He is very generous. He gives each of us way more than is necessary. So be generous right back.

You weren't an accident. You weren't mass-produced. You aren't an assembly-line product. You were deliberately planned, specifically gifted, and lovingly positioned on the earth by the Master Craftsman.
MAX LUCADO, PASTOR

GOD'S PROMISES
ABOUT GIFTS

He surrounds me with loving-kindness and tender
mercies. He fills my life with good things!
PSALM 103:4–5 TLB

Do not neglect the gift that is in you.
I TIMOTHY 4:14 NKJV

God has given each of you a gift
from His great variety of spiritual gifts.
Use them well to serve one another.
I PETER 4:10 NLT

There are different kinds of spiritual gifts,
but the same Spirit is the source of them all.
I CORINTHIANS 12:4 NLT

His lord said to him, "Well done, good and faithful
servant; you were faithful over a few things,
I will make you ruler over many things.
Enter into the joy of your lord."
MATTHEW 25:21 NKJV

36

GOD FIRST

In everything you do, put God first,
and He will direct you.
PROVERBS 3:6 TLB

In a crazy, uncertain world, there's one place with all the answers. Or more correctly, one Person.

God never lies. He never misses. He never predicts a thing and finds Himself having to back-pedal or explain Himself. God is no half-accurate weatherman!

Every word He speaks is true. Every word of His Word is true. And He promises that if we ask, we'll receive; if we seek, we'll find; if we knock, the door will be opened.

God doesn't always respond in the ways we expect or want. But anything we get from Him is right on the money.

The most important thing you must decide
to do every day is put the Lord first.
ELIZABETH GEORGE

GOD'S PROMISES ABOUT PUTTING HIM FIRST

You shall have no other gods before Me.
EXODUS 20:3 NKJV

Therefore, whether you eat or drink,
or whatever you do, do all to the glory of God.
I CORINTHIANS 10:31 NKJV

For this is the love of God,
that we keep His commandments.
And His commandments are not burdensome.
I JOHN 5:3 NKJV

How happy is everyone who fears the LORD,
who walks in His ways!
PSALM 128:1 HCSB

First we were loved, now we love. He loved us first.
I JOHN 4:19 THE MESSAGE

37

GOD'S LOVE

*The Lord still waits for you to come to Him,
so He can show you His love.*
ISAIAH 30:18 TLB

God is more than the inventor of love. He is more than the One who keeps love going. God is love. Every characteristic that can be applied to love can be applied to God. He is not rude or self-seeking. He is not easily angered. He keeps no record of wrongs.

When we love others, we're actually living out God's character. And when we are full of emotion, confused and hurt, and need to be reminded of how to love someone in that situation...we can examine God's character. We can mine First Corinthians 13 to look for help. And if we follow that way, we will never, ever go wrong.

*If you feel you are inadequate, worthless, or not
enough, you didn't get those ideas from God.*
LISA BEVERE, AUTHOR

GOD'S PROMISES
ABOUT HIS LOVE

Love is patient, love is kind.
Love does not envy, is not boastful, is not conceited,
does not act improperly, is not selfish, is not provoked,
and does not keep a record of wrongs.
I CORINTHIANS 13:4–5 HCSB

That's how much you mean to me!
That's how much I love you! I'd sell off the whole world
to get you back, trade the creation just for you.
ISAIAH 43:4 THE MESSAGE

But God showed His great love for us by sending
Christ to die for us while we were still sinners.
ROMANS 5:8 NLT

And we have known and believed the love that God
has for us. God is love, and he who abides in love
abides in God, and God in him.
I JOHN 4:16 NKJV

Let us, then, feel very sure that we can come before
God's throne where there is grace. There we can receive
mercy and grace to help us when we need it.
HEBREWS 4:16 NCV

38

GOD'S PLAN

*If you want to know what God wants you to do, ask
Him, and He will gladly tell you.*
JAMES 1:5 TLB

Indiana Jones needed to cross the 50-foot-wide chasm in *The Last Crusade* movie. He saw no way. But he had a clue: "Only in the lead from the lion's head...."

And so on faith, Indiana stuck his foot out. Shakily he stepped forward into nothingness...and landed on a beam. A previously invisible one, which carried him across to the other side.

We may not always see the power around us, but that doesn't mean it isn't there. The Lord often reveals His plan at the very moment we need to see it or else.

And this is faith. To believe that God is who He says He is. And believing is acting on what you know to be true, whether you see it or not.

*God is always doing 10,000 things in your life, and
you may be aware of three of them.*
JOHN PIPER, AUTHOR

GOD'S PROMISES
ABOUT HIS PLAN

We can make our plans,
but the final outcome is in God's hands.
PROVERBS 16:1 TLB

We confidently and joyfully look forward to actually
becoming all that God has had in mind for us to be.
ROMANS 5:2 TLB

"For I know the plans I have for you," says the LORD.
"They are plans for good and not for disaster, to give
you a future and a hope."
JEREMIAH 29:11 NLT

The Lord will work out His plans for my life—for Your
loving-kindness, Lord, continues forever.
PSALM 138:8 TLB

But as it is written: What eye did not see and ear did
not hear, and what never entered the human mind—
God prepared this for those who love Him.
I CORINTHIANS 2:9 HCSB

39

GOD'S PRESENCE

The one thing I want from God,
the thing I seek most of all, is the privilege of...
living in His presence every day of my life.
PSALM 27:4 TLB

"Who are you texting now? You've been on your phone all day!"

She rolls her eyes with a smile. "It's my dad. He's constantly checking on me. All he sends is emojis. Just dumb little reminders that he loves me."

And then the day came when she was in a car accident and her dad was the first one she called.

Because like an attentive dad, our Father is right there. All the time. Sending little reminders of His love. Some people call them His "kisses." And when we need Him most, calling on our Father is easier than hitting Send. "Because He's right there, waiting with bated breath, for us to remember His love.

If you have never known the power of God's love,
then maybe it is because you have never asked
to know it—I mean really asked,
expecting an answer.
FREDERICK BUECHNER, AUTHOR

GOD'S PROMISES
ABOUT HIS PRESENCE

The Lord your God is with you; the mighty One will
save you. He will rejoice over you. You will rest in His
love; He will sing and be joyful about you.
ZEPHANIAH 3:17 NCV

For the eyes of Yahweh roam throughout the earth
to show Himself strong for those whose hearts are
completely His.
II CHRONICLES 16:9 HCSB

Come close to God, and God will come close to you.
JAMES 4:8 NLT

I know the Lord is always with me. I will not be
shaken, for He is right beside me.
PSALM 16:8 NLT

I am not alone, because the Father is with Me.
JOHN 16:32 NKJV

40

GOD'S PROMISES

*But as it is written: What eye did not see and ear did
not hear, and what never entered the human mind—
God prepared this for those who love Him.*
I CORINTHIANS 2:9 HCSB

Science has a term called *hypothesis*: a theory to be
tested in order to determine its validity. A hypothesis is often called an "if/then statement." "If water is
brought to a temperature of 212 degrees, then it will
boil."

The Bible is full of if/then statements too. But
instead of theories, God's if/thens are promises. If we
ask, He will answer. If we believe, He will do it. If we
humble ourselves, He will hear us.

It couldn't be clearer: if we follow His ways, then
He will deliver on all His promises. If we draw near
to the Creator of the universe, accepting the truth of
Jesus, then we will have eternal life.

*Gather the riches of God's promises.
Nobody can take away from you those texts
from the Bible which you have learned by heart.*
CORRIE TEN BOOM, SURVIVOR

GOD'S PROMISES
ABOUT HIS PROMISES

*And we know that all things work together for good
to those who love God, to those who are the called
according to His purpose.*
ROMANS 8:28 NKJV

*So you'll go out in joy,
you'll be led into a whole and complete life.*
ISAIAH 55:12 The Message

*Let us hold on to the confession of our hope without
wavering, for He who promised is faithful.*
HEBREWS 10:23 HCSB

*Sustain me as You promised, and I will live;
do not let me be ashamed of my hope.*
PSALM 119:116 HCSB

*What a God! His road stretches straight and smooth.
Every GOD-direction is road-tested. Everyone who
runs toward Him makes it.*
PSALM 18:30 The Message

41

GOD'S SUPPORT

My grace is sufficient for you,
for My strength is made perfect in weakness.
II CORINTHIANS 12:9 NKJV

Princess movies are getting a bad rep these days. They can be seen as chauvinistic and unbalanced: the helpless maiden, trapped in a tower, needing rescue by the brave warrior prince.

But deep inside, we all need rescue. The tender, vulnerable part of us is crying out for hope and help. Movies and stories often reflect the deepest, loneliest parts of our hearts. We need our Savior!

No matter how tough or independent or strong you are, there's a tenderhearted child inside wanting a hero. This is nothing to be ashamed of. In fact, it is one of the sweetest gifts from God.

God's all-sufficiency is a major. Your inability is a
minor. Major in majors, not in minors.
CORRIE TEN BOOM

GOD'S PROMISES
ABOUT HIS SUPPORT

*You, O God, are both tender and kind, not easily
angered, immense in love, and you never, never quit.*
PSALM 86:15 THE MESSAGE

*Nevertheless God, who comforts the downcast,
comforted us.*
II CORINTHIANS 7:6 NKJV

*Therefore, we may boldly say: The Lord is my helper;
I will not be afraid. What can man do to me?*
HEBREWS 13:6 HCSB

*Therefore humble yourselves under the mighty hand
of God, that He may exalt you in due time, casting all
your care upon Him, for He cares for you.*
I PETER 5:6–7 NKJV

*The LORD is my light and my salvation—
whom should I fear? The LORD is the stronghold
of my life—of whom should I be afraid?*
PSALM 27:1 HCSB

42

GOD'S TIMING

Therefore humble yourselves under the mighty hand
of God, that He may exalt you in due time.
I PETER 5:6 NKJV

This is a right-now culture. Unlike our parents' and grandparents' generations, meals that take longer than 30 minutes to cook are almost unheard of. And just imagine waiting more than 5 minutes for a burger at the nearest fast-food restaurant! Waiting is not a gift that comes naturally to most of us.

But God's world is a patience culture. There is so much to look forward to, far beyond anything we could dare to ask or imagine. There will be a day when His faithful people will be rewarded beyond belief.

It just means that now, we wait. We live. Get to know Him as He is, follow faithfully, love others, and dream of the life to come. Just know this—it's going to be good!

With God, there's always an appointed time for
things, and when you put Him first, trust in His
timing, and keep the faith, miracles happen!
GERMANY KENT, JOURNALIST AND MODEL

GOD'S PROMISES
ABOUT HIS TIMING

Wait patiently for the LORD.
Be brave and courageous.
PSALM 27:14 NLT

God made everything beautiful in itself
and in its time.
ECCLESIASTES 3:11 THE MESSAGE

The LORD wants to show His mercy to you.
He wants to rise and comfort you.
The LORD is a fair God, and everyone
who waits for His help will be happy.
ISAIAH 30:18 NCV

Trust in the LORD with all your heart, and lean
not on your own understanding; in all your ways
acknowledge Him, and He shall direct your paths.
PROVERBS 3:5-6 NKJV

For everything there is a season,
a time for every activity under heaven.
ECCLESIASTES 3:1 NLT

43

HAPPINESS

Happiness makes a person smile,
but sadness can break a person's spirit.
PROVERBS 15:13 NCV

As defined in Webster's Dictionary (1828), rejoice means to "experience joy and gladness in a high degree; to be exhilarated with lively and pleasurable sensations; to exult." Wow, what a life we're expected to lead! One with high levels of joy and gladness, with exhilaration and pleasure mixed in. Not too shabby!

If you're like most people, most of your life is not lived at a high level of exhilaration. So many distractions and opportunities to worry about. So much hurt.

Only the grace of God can bring us to a place where rejoicing is an everyday, every-moment way of life. But it is possible. Because He says so. If you want to live a happy life, ask Him to show you the way. Sooner than you think, you'll be dancing.

You are most yourself when you are wrapped up
in your purpose, not your position.
STEFFANY GRETZINGER, WORSHIP LEADER

GOD'S PROMISES
ABOUT HAPPINESS

The ways of right-living people glow with light;
the longer they live, the brighter they shine.
PROVERBS 4:18 THE MESSAGE

Those who listen to instruction will prosper;
those who trust the LORD will be joyful.
PROVERBS 16:20 NLT

If they obey and serve Him,
they'll have a good, long life on easy street.
JOB 36:11 THE MESSAGE

I have come that they may have life,
and that they may have it more abundantly.
JOHN 10:10 NKJV

Joyful is the person who finds wisdom,
the one who gains understanding.
PROVERBS 3:13 NLT

44

HELPING OTHERS

Whenever you are able,
do good to people who need help.
PROVERBS 3:27 NCV

He knew it was dangerous. Lethal, even. But he just had this feeling that it was his calling. So the missionary doctor turned away from all the desperate pleas and advice from home and walked right into the diseased masses. Anyone who got near the patients would be expected to contract the disease—with a 24-hour life expectancy—within two days. But he had the Holy Spirit with him, and he believed.

Years later, the doctor spoke of his experience. "I'm not a hero. I'm very weak. But in my weakness He is strong, and that strengthens me."

We're not all anointed against communicable diseases.
But you do have a special calling on your life.
How has God gifted you to uniquely serve others?
No one has ever become poor by giving.
ANNE FRANK, DIARIST

GOD'S PROMISES ABOUT
HELPING OTHERS

You're blessed when you care. At the moment of being
"care-full," you find yourselves cared for.
MATTHEW 5:7 THE MESSAGE

Carry one another's burdens;
in this way you will fulfill the law of Christ.
GALATIANS 6:2 HCSB

So let's not get tired of doing what is good.
At just the right time we will reap
a harvest of blessing if we don't give up.
GALATIANS 6:9 NLT

If you have two shirts, give one to the poor.
If you have food, share it with those who are hungry.
LUKE 3:11 NLT

Whatever you did for
one of the least of these brothers of Mine,
you did for Me.
MATTHEW 25:40 HCSB

45

HOPE

This hope we have as an anchor of the soul,
a hope both sure and steadfast.
HEBREWS 6:19 NASB

It's most likely that if you are in need of groceries, you get in the car and head to the nearest store (or ask someone you love to go for you). If you want to see a movie, you either turn on the TV or look up a new release at the local theater.

It makes good sense that when we need hope, we go to the Source of all hope. Hope is God's specialty. He invented it. When things looked bleak, Jesus came along bearing all the possibility of freedom and eternal life. And it didn't end at the cross. Hope is a necessary part of life. It fills and sustains us. And we're meant to share it with the world around us. So go to the Source today and get you some hope!

Sometimes when you're in a dark place, you think
you've been buried, but you've actually been planted.
CHRISTINE CAINE, ACTIVIST

GOD'S PROMISES
ABOUT HOPE

Then you will know that I am the LORD.
Those who trust in Me will never be put to shame.
ISAIAH 49:23 NLT

Let us hold fast the confession of our hope without
wavering, for He who promised is faithful.
HEBREWS 10:23 NASB

I say to myself, "The LORD is mine, so I hope in Him."
LAMENTATIONS 3:24 NCV

The LORD is good to those who wait for Him, to the
soul who seeks Him. It is good that one should hope
and wait quietly for the salvation of the LORD.
LAMENTATIONS 3:25–26 NKJV

Be strong and courageous,
all you who put your hope in the LORD.
PSALM 31:24 HCSB

46

HUMILITY

Sometimes our humble hearts can help us
more than our proud minds.
I CORINTHIANS 8:2 THE MESSAGE

A wise worship leader once gave this advice: "Live a lifestyle of repentance." Does that mean constantly beating yourself up, punishing yourself, or recalling all the things you've done wrong lately? Of course not!

Repentance is a change of mind, or a 180-degree turn from sin toward God. A lifestyle of repentance involves constantly adjusting course toward God and away from sin. Sin separates us from God. So repentance means breaking down those walls by receiving His forgiveness and determining to change behavior so that you won't be in that position again.

The mercy of God is there for the taking, if you're willing to humbly take your place at His feet.

The mercy of God is there for the taking,
if you're willing to humbly take your place at His feet.
When we come out of our darkness into the light of Jesus
Christ, we become broken by our sins. It is our humble
repentance that turns us toward the Light.
It is our need of Him that draws us to the Light.
Our only covering is His righteousness—
our only hope is His mercy.
ROY LESSIN, AUTHOR

GOD'S PROMISES
ABOUT HUMILITY

If you think you know it all, you're a fool for sure;
real survivors learn wisdom from others.
PROVERBS 28:26 THE MESSAGE

I can do everything through Christ,
who gives me strength.
PHILIPPIANS 4:13 NLT

Let the wise listen to these proverbs
and become even wiser.
Let those with understanding receive guidance.
PROVERBS 1:5 NLT

Therefore most gladly I will rather boast
in my infirmities, that the power of Christ
may rest upon me.
II CORINTHIANS 12:9 NKJV

Whoever becomes simple and elemental again,
like this child, will rank high in God's kingdom.
MATTHEW 18:4 THE MESSAGE

47

JOY

The joy of the Lord is your strength.
NEHEMIAH 8:10 TLB

The truth is, Jesus is enough. He is enough when you don't know what to do. He has the answers. Or when you're on the best vacation of your life, it is wonderful—but still less fulfilling than the fullness of Jesus. Measure everything by His standard: total acceptance, absolute joy, complete fulfillment, and unending love. What could possibly compare to any of that alone, never mind all together?

Take the joy of Jesus with you, and it will keep the rest of life in perspective. His joy allows you to weather a storm, comfort a friend, and truly enjoy a celebration. When you have Jesus, you have all the confidence in the world to live in joy.

Joy is serious business of heaven.
C. S. LEWIS, THEOLOGIAN

GOD'S PROMISES
ABOUT JOY

Now all glory to God, who is able to keep you from
falling away and will bring you with great joy into
His glorious presence without a single fault.
JUDE 1:24 NLT

He will yet fill your mouth with laughing,
and your lips with rejoicing.
JOB 8:21 NKJV

Rejoice in the Lord always.
Again I will say, rejoice!
PHILIPPIANS 4:4 NKJV

Until now you have asked for nothing in My name.
Ask and you will receive,
so that your joy may be complete.
JOHN 16:24 HCSB

So you also have sorrow now.
But I will see you again. Your hearts will rejoice,
and no one will rob you of your joy.
JOHN 16:22 HCSB

48

JUDGING OTHERS

Therefore, any one of you who judges is without excuse. For when you judge another, you condemn yourself, since you, the judge, do the same things.
ROMANS 2:1 HCSB

Tattoos have become much more mainstream. Jesus has always said, "Come as you are; I can work with it!" But more commonly than ever, even believers are ending up inked. Same with piercings and the occasional craft beer. What are we to think of this? Is it unbiblical? Does it offend God? Should it offend us?

It's easy to see what's seeable, and that's where a person's mind dwells. But the mind of God searches the heart of mankind—in places no human can see. A person gives off truer signals about their spiritual needs than just by the visible. Watch behaviors and words more than pierced eyebrows or inked arms—and you may begin to spot the needs worth going after.

To judge someone is to say that I have the right to define who they are, versus understanding that God has handed me the priceless privilege of discovering who they are.
CRAIG D. LOUNSBROUGH, COUNSELOR

GOD'S PROMISES ABOUT JUDGING OTHERS

*See to it that you really do love each other warmly,
with all your hearts.*
I PETER 1:22 TLB

*Don't speak evil against each other, dear brothers and
sisters. If you criticize and judge each other, then you
are criticizing and judging God's law. But your job is
to obey the law, not to judge whether it applies to you.*
JAMES 4:11 NLT

*Do everything without grumbling and arguing,
so that you may be blameless and pure.*
PHILIPPIANS 2:14-15 HCSB

*Those who control their tongue will have a long life;
opening your mouth can ruin everything.*
PROVERBS 13:3 NLT

*Don't pick on people, jump on their failures, criticize
their faults—unless, of course, you want the same
treatment. Don't condemn those who are down; that
hardness can boomerang. Be easy on people; you'll
find life a lot easier.*
LUKE 6:37 THE MESSAGE

49

KINDNESS AND COMPASSION

Be kind to one another, tenderhearted,
forgiving one another, even as God in Christ
forgave you.
EPHESIANS 4:32 NKJV

There's no trickery in God. He's not the kind of leader who says one thing and does another. He always honors a pure heart. He rewards the faithful, and shows His kindness to generation after generation. You'll never have to worry about being deceived or rejected. Nothing you've done will scare the Lord off or cause Him to punish you. God loves you as you are, blemishes and all.

He looks at the aim of your life and judges based on that. Are you aiming toward Jesus? Success! Are you off base? He'll nudge you right. Are you lost? He'll come find you. His goodness is incomparable.

Don't treat people the way they treat you.
Treat people the way God treats you.
DAVE WILLIS, PASTOR

GOD'S PROMISES ABOUT KINDNESS AND COMPASSION

Tell me in the morning about Your love,
because I trust You. Show me what I should do,
because my prayers go up to You.
PSALM 143:8 NCV

May God who gives patience, steadiness,
and encouragement help you to live
in complete harmony with each other.
ROMANS 15:5 TLB

And let us not grow weary while doing good, for in
due season we shall reap if we do not lose heart.
GALATIANS 6:9 NKJV

Whenever you did one of these things
to someone overlooked or ignored, that was Me—
you did it to Me.
MATTHEW 25:40 The Message

50

KINGDOM WEALTH

*Every good gift and every perfect gift is from above,
and comes down from the Father of lights.*
JAMES 1:17 NKJV

A pauper lives like as if next meal is unsure. He stores away his money, unable to share and afraid to spend. His friendships are guarded and distant: "what if they needed or asked something of me? I can't afford to give!" He needs more than he gives.

A prince (or princess) lives as if the next meal will surely satisfy him. He invests his money wisely and makes giving part of his budget. His friendships are open and fruitful: "Am I the very best, most welcoming person I can be? I can't wait to give today!" He serves more than he expects.

God is the God of abundance. Do you doubt that (pauper) or believe it (prince)?

*Abundance isn't God's provision for me to live in
luxury. It's His provision for me to help others live.
God entrusts me with His money, not to build
my kingdom on earth, but to build
His kingdom in heaven.*
RANDY ALCORN, AUTHOR

GOD'S PROMISES ABOUT KINGDOM WEALTH

God will lavish you with good things.
DEUTERONOMY 28:11 THE MESSAGE

*Remember that the Lord will give you
an inheritance as your reward,
and that the Master you are serving is Christ.*
COLOSSIANS 3:24 NLT

*Give away your life; you'll find life given back,
but not merely given back—given back with bonus
and blessing. Giving, not getting, is the way.
Generosity begets generosity.*
LUKE 6:38 THE MESSAGE

*The generous will prosper; those who refresh others
will themselves be refreshed.*
PROVERBS 11:25 NLT

*Even though you are bad, you know how to give good
gifts to your children. How much more your heavenly
Father will give good things to those who ask Him!*
MATTHEW 7:11 NCV

51

LEARNING

A wise man will hear and increase learning,
and a man of understanding will attain wise counsel.
PROVERBS 1:5 NKJV

Schoolteachers and medical doctors have something in common: continuing education. If a doctor stopped learning after med school, then twenty years later her knowledge would fall short of the newer diseases and treatments. Things could get dangerous. Fast!

Staying connected to the Source of all knowledge and wisdom is a must for believers. He is generous with what He has. But you have to be in a position to receive. If you do, you'll bear the sweetest, most helpful fruit.

Get and stay in tune with the Holy Spirit, your glue for remaining in the Vine.

Don't be normal. Be an example.
TIM TEBOW, ATHLETE

GOD'S PROMISES
ABOUT LEARNING

Listen to advice and accept correction,
and in the end you will be wise.
PROVERBS 19:20 NCV

Get wisdom—it's worth more than money;
choose insight over income every time.
PROVERBS 16:16 THE MESSAGE

Those who are wise shall shine like the brightness
of the firmament, and those who turn many to
righteousness like the stars forever and ever.
DANIEL 12:3 NKJV

Iron sharpens iron,
and one man sharpens another.
PROVERBS 27:17 HCSB

A fool's way is right in his own eyes,
but whoever listens to counsel is wise.
PROVERBS 12:15 HCSB

52

MIRACLES

*I tell you the truth, anyone who believes in Me will do
the same works I have done, and even greater works,
because I am going to be with the Father.*
JOHN 14:12 NLT

Everyday miracles. Are there even such things?
Can any supernatural occurrence be considered
ordinary?

But many miracles of God are very subtle. Like
the way He brings two people together in love and
knits them together for fifty years or more. Without
the Lord, human beings just don't get along that well!
Or the way a flower grows. Have you ever studied the
perfect symmetry of a flower, repeated over and over
again in similar colors and sizes? That is no accident!

We become accustomed to the ways that the Lord
constantly, consistently provides miracles. But spend
any time considering what would not be possible
without God and you'll be in awe again and again.

*Are you missing your miracle
because you're calling it coincidence?*
STEVEN FURTICK, PASTOR

GOD'S PROMISES
ABOUT MIRACLES

Is anything too hard for the LORD?
GENESIS 18:14 NKJV

And God confirmed the message by giving signs and wonders and various miracles and gifts of the Holy Spirit whenever He chose.
HEBREWS 2:4 NLT

No one's ever seen or heard anything like this, never so much as imagined anything quite like it— what God has arranged for those who love Him.
I CORINTHIANS 2:9 THE MESSAGE

You are the God of great wonders! You demonstrate Your awesome power among the nations.
PSALM 77:14 NLT

God can do anything!
LUKE 1:37 NCV

53

MISTAKES

If we confess our sins to Him,
He is faithful and just to forgive us
and to cleanse us from all wickedness.
I JOHN 1:9 NLT

The drippy mess sits there on the sidewalk, sagging as it melts in the summer sun. Above the blob, a small hand. In the hand, an empty ice cream cone. Above the cone, a quivering lip and two doe eyes filling to the brim as they search your face in despair.

Are you angry that your young niece dropped her ice cream? Will you scold her for being careless? Or does your heart melt just a little bit along with that strawberry mess, as you take your niece's hand and head back to the parlor for a fresh scoop—maybe in a cup this time?

God's mercy is indescribable and His tolerance so merciful. He loves our innocence and understands our current level of maturity.

Our mess is the canvas on which God paints
His story of redemption.
LOUIE GIGLIO, PASTOR

GOD'S PROMISES
ABOUT MISTAKES

He who covers his sins will not prosper, but whoever
confesses and forsakes them will have mercy.
PROVERBS 28:13 NKJV

Therefore let us approach the throne of grace
with boldness, so that we may receive mercy
and find grace to help us at the proper time.
HEBREWS 4:16 HCSB

GOD's love, though, is ever and always,
eternally present to all who fear Him,
making everything right for them and their children.
PSALM 103:17 THE MESSAGE

You must be compassionate,
just as your Father is compassionate.
LUKE 6:36 NLT

Therefore, if anyone is in Christ,
he is a new creation; old things have passed away;
behold, all things have become new.
II CORINTHIANS 5:17 NKJV

54

MOTIVES

People may be right in their own eyes,
but the Lord examines their heart.
PROVERBS 21:2 NLT

Imagine being accused of plagiarism. The professor and principal are prepared to suspend you based on circumstantial evidence. But you know that you worked all weekend to write the paper in your own words! How easy would it be for you to stay quiet and take the punishment when injustice is being served?

We've been wired to want what is right for ourselves and the ones we love. There's nothing wrong with that! But above getting justice, the most important thing is having true and pure motives. When you know you've acted with integrity, then what others believe is less important. The Lord looks at the heart and knows the truth.

You may or may not see justice for all things on this earth before you die. But you can be sure that God keeps track of motives, and He executes perfect justice. Whatever you leave in His hands will be handled in the very best way.

If you would test the character of anything,
you only need to inquire whether that thing
leads you to God or away from God.
WATCHMAN NEE, TEACHER

GOD'S PROMISES
ABOUT MOTIVES

Do you think I speak this strongly in order to manipulate crowds? Or curry favor with God? Or get popular applause? If my goal was popularity, I wouldn't bother being Christ's slave.
GALATIANS 1:10 THE MESSAGE

But as we have been approved by God to be entrusted with the gospel, even so we speak, not as pleasing men, but God who tests our hearts.
I THESSALONIANS 2:4 NKJV

Do nothing out of rivalry or conceit, but in humility consider others as more important than yourselves.
PHILIPPIANS 2:3 HCSB

That all believers would be filled with love that comes from a pure heart, a clear conscience, and genuine faith.
I TIMOTHY 1:5 NLT

All the ways of a man are pure in his own eyes, but the LORD weighs the spirits.
PROVERBS 16:2 NKJV

55

OBEDIENCE

Just tell me what to do and I will do it, Lord.
As long as I live I'll wholeheartedly obey.
PSALM 119:33–34 TLB

There's a reward that comes from simply hanging in there. Recipients of this reward don't earn it by running fast or being the best. Sometimes the race that gets them there is less than graceful: like a kitten slipping from a branch and clinging to the bark with two splayed and desperate paws. Hang in there long enough, and the hero fireman will come to the rescue. And you'll end up cuddled close in the arms of the One who loves you.

The "hang in there" reward comes to those who simply don't give up in life. They get up each day planning to take just the next step of obedience toward God. They may fall down again and again, but they always get up and keep aiming toward Jesus.

God is awesome;
He doesn't need you to be awesome.
He wants you to be obedient.
MATT CHANDLER, PASTOR

GOD'S PROMISES ABOUT OBEDIENCE

Now by this we know that we know Him,
if we keep His commandments.
I JOHN 2:3 NKJV

We must obey God rather than men.
ACTS 5:29 NASB

Praise the LORD! Happy are those who respect
the LORD, who want what He commands.
PSALM 112:1 NCV

But prove yourselves doers of the word,
and not merely hearers who delude themselves.
JAMES 1:22 NASB

Trust in the LORD with all your heart, and lean
not on your own understanding; in all your ways
acknowledge Him, and He shall direct your paths.
PROVERBS 3:5–6 NKJV

56

PARTNERSHIP

When you draw close to God,
God will draw close to you.
JAMES 4:8 TLB

It can be overwhelming to see all the need around us every day. Kids who don't eat unless schools provide lunches. Veterans with broken bodies, minds, or hearts. Young girls and boys kidnapped and used in the sex trade. A person can feel useless and pointless in the midst of such need.

The Lord thought ahead to this problem. He knows the needs. And He prepared your set of needs even before you were born. He knows where He wants you.

So how do you figure out where He wants you? Stay in tune. Be His partner. Pay attention to the things that stir your heart in a special way. Then go out in joy and serve. He will show you the way.

Real joy comes when we get the right desire met—
the desire for God Himself, for a life led by the Spirit,
fulfilling not our material desires but our deepest
need, which is to be in a close relationship with our
Creator. That is the source of true blessing.
The only source.
MICHAEL W. SMITH, MUSICIAN

GOD'S PROMISES
ABOUT PARTNERSHIP

Each morning I will look to You in heaven
and lay my requests before You.
PSALM 5:3 TLB

I also tell you this: If two of you agree
here on earth concerning anything you ask,
My Father in heaven will do it for you.
MATTHEW 18:19 NLT

For it is God who works in you both to will
and to do for His good pleasure.
PHILIPPIANS 2:13 NKJV

It's not the one who plants or the one who waters
who is at the center of this process but God,
who makes things grow.
I CORINTHIANS 3:7 THE MESSAGE

For we are God's coworkers.
You are God's field, God's building.
I CORINTHIANS 3:9 HCSB

57

PAST

*Do not remember the former things, nor consider the
things of old. Behold, I will do a new thing.*
ISAIAH 43:18–19 NKJV

What's done is done. The past is past. If it was
good, relish in the completion of it. If it was
bad, be thankful that the blood of Jesus covers all.
But there's just way too much now to spend time worrying about then. Focus on what is going on around
you and how you fit into it all. There's so much
opportunity within your current reach, and you don't
want to miss it!

The beautiful thing is, the more you dwell in the
present with the Lord, the more it sets you up for the
future He has planned for you. So the only tense you
need to focus on today is the present.

*It is no use to pray for the old days; stand square
where you are and make the present
better than any past has been.*
OSWALD CHAMBERS, TEACHER

GOD'S PROMISES
ABOUT THE PAST

*One thing I do, forgetting those things which are
behind and reaching forward to those things which
are ahead, I press toward the goal for the prize
of the upward call of God in Christ Jesus.*
PHILIPPIANS 3:13–14 NKJV

*Have mercy on me, O God, because of Your unfailing
love. Because of Your great compassion,
blot out the stain of my sins. Wash me clean
from my guilt. Purify me from my sin.*
PSALM 51:1–2 NLT

*Your old sinful self has died,
and your new life is kept with Christ in God.*
COLOSSIANS 3:3 NCV

*True to Your word, You let me catch my breath
and send me in the right direction.*
PSALM 23:3 THE MESSAGE

58

PATIENCE

Better to be patient than powerful;
better to have self-control than to conquer a city.
PROVERBS 16:32 NLT

It was her second time behind the wheel—a stick shift, no less—and she kept killing the engine. "Mom, I'll never get this right! I'm a horrible driver!"

"Honey, you are fifteen years old, and you are learning. You are at the exact level of driving ability that you're supposed to be! You'll get better!"

The end is not the goal for everyday life. The journey is! Where you are today is where God wants you. He's growing you, maturing you, and bringing you to completion over time.

God works at different paces, in different ways, with every person. Focus on your own adventure, and you'll get the most out of it as you go.

The devil doesn't know what to do with somebody
who just won't give up.
JOYCE MEYER, AUTHOR

GOD'S PROMISES ABOUT PATIENCE

It pays to take life seriously;
things work out when you trust in GOD.
PROVERBS 16:20 THE MESSAGE

It is better to finish something than to start it.
It is better to be patient than to be proud.
ECCLESIASTES 7:8 NCV

But if we look forward to something we don't yet have,
we must wait patiently and confidently.
ROMANS 8:25 NLT

The LORD is good to those who depend on Him, to
those who search for Him. So it is good to wait quietly
for salvation from the LORD.
LAMENTATIONS 3:25–26 NLT

Rejoice in our confident hope. Be patient in trouble,
and keep on praying.
ROMANS 12:12 NLT

59

POPULARITY

*For am I now trying to win the favor of people, or
God? Or am I striving to please people?
If I were still trying to please people,
I would not be a slave of Christ.*
GALATIANS 1:10 HCSB

Forget your station. Forget your title. Forget what you're wearing today, who knows you exist, how much money you make, or what kind of bicycle you ride.

At the core, we are all sheep. We all flock together. We all follow the same Shepherd. Some of us wear wool suits, and some of us wear woolen underwear. But wool is wool, and once in a while we are all subject to being shorn.

Do you think that in a real flock, much time is spent comparing nose color or hoof size or who is eating the better patch of grass? No! Every sheep has its place in the Shepherd's presence. Life is good, when you're a sheep in the kingdom of God.

*We won't be distracted by comparison
if we are captivated with purpose.*
BOB GOFF, AUTHOR

GOD'S PROMISES
ABOUT POPULARITY

The fear of man is a snare,
but the one who trusts in the LORD is protected.
PROVERBS 29:25 HCSB

It is better to take refuge in the LORD
than to trust in people.
PSALM 118:8 NLT

Dear friend, if bad companions tempt you,
don't go along with them.
PROVERBS 1:10 THE MESSAGE

Keep your eyes straight ahead;
ignore all sideshow distractions.
PROVERBS 4:25 THE MESSAGE

Do not be unequally yoked together with unbelievers.
For what fellowship has righteousness
with lawlessness? And what communion
has light with darkness?
II CORINTHIANS 6:14 NKJV

60

PRAISE

Let everything that breathes praise the LORD.
Hallelujah!
PSALM 150:6 HCSB

God is full of wise advice. He's not in the business of puffing Himself up for His own sake, but He knows and wants the very best for us.

That's why, when He says praise and thanks are good medicine, you can believe it. Maybe you've experienced it before. You're having a terrible day. And in a moment of clarity you decide to focus on the good things. You think of things to be thankful for. You turn your thanks toward God. Pretty soon, the more you focus on His goodness, the better you feel.

The Bible actually tells us to dance, sing, and praise Him! There are times to be quiet and stoic. There are also times to lavish God with extravagant praise.

It is more difficult to find the Creator in a barbecue sandwich than in your favorite Sunday-morning song, but when you do, when you begin to find Him in all the stuff of life, everything starts singing. Every moment breaks into song. Every breath becomes sacrifice, and the songs become sweetness. This is living praise.
DAVID CROWDER, MUSICIAN

GOD'S PROMISES
ABOUT PRAISE

All of you can join together
with one voice, giving praise and glory to God,
the Father of our Lord Jesus Christ.
ROMANS 15:6 NLT

How we praise God, the Father of our Lord Jesus
Christ, who has blessed us with every blessing in
heaven because we belong to Christ.
EPHESIANS 1:3 TLB

Great is the LORD! He is most worthy of praise!
No one can measure His greatness.
PSALM 145:3 NLT

In everything give thanks;
for this is the will of God in Christ Jesus for you.
I THESSALONIANS 5:18 NKJV

The LORD is my strength and my song;
He has become my salvation.
EXODUS 15:2 HCSB

61

PRAYER

When I pray, You answer me and encourage me
by giving me the strength I need.
PSALM 138:3 TLB

Sometimes things happen just so God can show us who He really is. Sometimes we end up in situations that are tailor-made for our cries out to Him for help and understanding. Then, when He delivers, it's so obvious where the help came from!

How often do people forget to call on God in times of need? How often do we try to do things under our own steam, only to give up defeated and exhausted?

The next time you find yourself striving, try dropping everything and crying out to Him. He may just have the answer you've been waiting for.

Prayer is of transcendent importance.
Prayer is the mightiest agent to advance God's work.
Praying hearts and hands only can do God's work.
Prayer succeeds when all else fails.
E. M. BOUNDS, AUTHOR

GOD'S PROMISES
ABOUT PRAYER

Whatever God says to us is full of living power.
HEBREWS 4:12 TLB

*The earnest prayer of a righteous person
has great power and produces wonderful results.*
JAMES 5:16 NLT

*God answered their prayers
because they trusted Him.*
I CHRONICLES 5:20 THE MESSAGE

*Rejoice always, pray without ceasing,
in everything give thanks;
for this is the will of God in Christ Jesus for you.*
I THESSALONIANS 5:16–18 NKJV

*Ask, and it will be given to you;
seek, and you will find;
knock, and it will be opened to you.
For every one who asks receives,
and he who seeks finds,
and to him who knocks it will be opened.*
MATTHEW 7:7–8 NASB

62

PRIORITIES

For where your treasure is,
there your heart will be also.
LUKE 12:34 HCSB

I f you've ever cheated on a test (no, of course not, right?) you know that the reward isn't quite as sweet as working hard and doing your very best.

Life isn't meant to be cheated, although there are lots of ways to cut corners! No text message could ever compete with showing up for a friend's graduation party or coming to a memorial service and giving that hug of sympathy and sorrow.

The easy way isn't always the best way, and the best way isn't always hard. The trick is to stay focused on Jesus and walk where He walks. If you do, you'll definitely benefit from the reward of walking well.

Wisdom, priorities, adventure, loving and being
loved, the sustaining power of faith...
the legacy of a life well-invested in things
that really matter.
MATT ANDERSON, WRITER

GOD'S PROMISES ABOUT PRIORITIES

Therefore, whether you eat or drink,
or whatever you do, do everything for God's glory.
I CORINTHIANS 10:31 HCSB

Trust GOD from the bottom of your heart;
don't try to figure out everything on your own.
PROVERBS 3:5 THE MESSAGE

Make yourself an example of good works
with integrity and dignity in your teaching.
TITUS 2:7 HCSB

But prove yourselves doers of the word,
and not merely hearers who delude themselves.
JAMES 1:22 NASB

63

PURPOSE

*You saw me before I was born and scheduled each day
of my life before I began to breathe.*
PSALM 139:16 TLB

A quiltmaker has the finished design in mind as she begins her work. As she chooses fabrics, patterns, and colors, she knows where she's headed. It's the end result that inspires her through the work of planning and stitching and cutting.

God knew where He was headed when He knitted you together. He had your whole life dreamed up. As He (who could snap you together in a moment) patiently formed your body over days and months, He daydreamed about who you would become. He looked forward to the very day you would choose to believe in Jesus. He smiled at the joy you would bring. And He put you together perfectly, piece by loving piece at a time. You, friend, are very much on purpose.

*You can't be who you're going to be
and who you used to be at the same time.*
BISHOP T. D. JAKES

GOD'S PROMISES
ABOUT PURPOSE

I chose you! I appointed you to go
and produce lovely fruit.
JOHN 15:16 TLB

We have also received an inheritance in Him,
predestined according to the purpose of the
One who works out everything in agreement
with the decision of His will.
EPHESIANS 1:11 HCSB

For we are God's coworkers.
You are God's field, God's building.
I CORINTHIANS 3:9 HCSB

And whatever you do, do it heartily,
as to the Lord and not to men.
COLOSSIANS 3:23 NKJV

For we are His creation, created in Christ Jesus for
good works, which God prepared ahead of time
so that we should walk in them.
EPHESIANS 2:10 HCSB

64

PURSUIT

*Whoever pursues righteousness and unfailing love
will find life, righteousness, and honor.*
PROVERBS 21:21 NLT

Jesus has a habit of enlisting the least-prepared,
least-expected people. Not because He's a bad
judge of character, but because He's the best! He sees
potential, adds the necessary training, and trans-
forms the weak into ministers of His grace.

And it doesn't stop after boot camp! Jesus is into
"continuing education." He remains a mentor for
life, leading His people through Holy Spirit courses
on love, joy, peace, patience, kindness, goodness,
faithfulness, gentleness, and self-control (Gal 5:22–
23). It's a comprehensive program, designed to bring
you to completion in Him one day. So if you're a
student, you're in the very best hands. Take courage
that Jesus believes in you!

*We never grow closer to God when we just live life.
It takes deliberate pursuit and attentiveness.*
FRANCIS CHAN, PASTOR

GOD'S PROMISES
ABOUT PURSUIT

Don't ever forget kindness and truth.
Wear them like a necklace.
Write them on your heart as if on a tablet.
PROVERBS 3:3 NCV

Happy are those who long to be just and good,
for they shall be completely satisfied.
MATTHEW 5:6 TLB

If you look for Me wholeheartedly,
you will find Me.
JEREMIAH 29:13 NLT

Snub evil and cultivate good;
run after peace for all you're worth.
I PETER 3:11 The Message

I pursue as my goal the prize promised
by God's heavenly call in Christ Jesus.
PHILIPPIANS 3:14 HCSB

65

QUIET TIME

Be still, and know that I am God;
I will be exalted among the nations,
I will be exalted in the earth!
PSALM 46:10 NKJV

Preventive medicine can save a person a lot of heartache (or headache or any other body ache)! Letting a doctor check for trouble can keep you much healthier in the long run.

Spending time with God through prayer, listening, reading the Word, and many other ways can get you ready for anything that comes along. Taking Him seriously builds your trust in what He says and who He is. It's kind of like adding tools to your tool chest, just in case. You never know what life will bring, and being as ready as possible by knowing Him as well as you can will bring a whole lot of peace when you get there.

It is in that stillness that the Voice will be heard,
the only voice in all the universe that speaks
peace to the deepest part of us.
ELISABETH ELLIOT, AUTHOR

GOD'S PROMISES
ABOUT QUIET TIME

*Now in the morning, having risen a long while
before daylight, He went out and departed
to a solitary place; and there He prayed.*
MARK 1:35 NKJV

*Truly my soul silently waits for God;
from Him comes my salvation.*
PSALM 62:1 NKJV

Listen in silence before Me.
ISAIAH 41:1 NLT

In quietness and confidence is your strength.
ISAIAH 30:15 NLT

*There is an occasion for everything...
a time to be silent and a time to speak.*
ECCLESIASTES 3:1, 7 HCSB

66

RISK

Don't be afraid, for the Lord will go before you
and will be with you;
He will not fail nor forsake you.
DEUTERONOMY 31:8 TLB

The dog shivered in the backyard cage. She was scared, emaciated, and weatherworn. The rescuers gathered her and transported her to safety. They named her Joy.

Daily, Dr. Villa stepped inside Joy's cage with a bowl of food. He sat at the far end and waited. Joy stayed in her corner at first. Little by little, she began inching forward on paws and elbows—one day to sniff the food, one day to eat it, and one day to crawl past the empty bowl toward the doctor. It wasn't until Joy's nose touched Dr. Villa's knee one day that he touched her back. And that was the beginning of Joy's true rehabilitation into love.

God waits until we're ready to risk everything. But when we move, He moves.

You'll never reach second base
if you keep one foot on first.
VERNON LAW, BASEBALL PITCHER

GOD'S PROMISES ABOUT RISK

*For He will order His angels to protect you wherever
you go. They will hold you up with their hands
so you won't even hurt your foot on a stone.*
PSALM 91:11–12 NLT

*A prudent person foresees danger and takes
precautions. The simpleton goes blindly on
and suffers the consequences.*
PROVERBS 22:3 NLT

*But those who are noble make noble plans,
and stand for what is noble.*
ISAIAH 32:8 THE MESSAGE

*Commit your actions to the LORD,
and your plans will succeed.*
PROVERBS 16:3 NLT

*Spend time with the wise
and you will become wise.*
PROVERBS 13:20 NCV

67

SERVICE AND SERVING GOD

He who is greatest among you shall be your servant.
And whoever exalts himself will be humbled, and he
who humbles himself will be exalted.
MATTHEW 23:11–12 NKJV

You can read all the books. Take all the classes. Watch all the others doing it. But until you find yourself challenged to love the unlovable, such a thing will only be a concept. It's easy to love when the feelings are there. But what about when it's the last thing you feel like doing?

Getting to know Jesus means benefiting from the purest love known to man. And as that experience washes over you, it won't be long before you are so full yourself that loving others will be an act of love to Jesus, your very favorite.

Serving others through a love for Jesus makes loving
the unlovable a whole lot easier—and very rewarding.
When you feel down, go be a blessing to somebody else.
JOYCE MEYER, AUTHOR

GOD'S PROMISES ABOUT SERVICE AND SERVING HIM

In response to all He has done for us,
let us outdo each other in being helpful and kind.
HEBREWS 10:24 TLB

Live out your God-created identity.
Live generously and graciously toward others,
the way God lives toward you.
MATTHEW 5:48 THE MESSAGE

Shepherd God's flock, for whom you are responsible.
Watch over them because you want to,
not because you are forced.
That is how God wants it.
Do it because you are happy to serve.
I PETER 5:2 NCV

As each one has received a gift,
minister it to one another, as good stewards
of the manifold grace of God.
I PETER 4:10 NKJV

Isn't it obvious that God-talk without God-acts
is outrageous nonsense?
JAMES 2:17 THE MESSAGE

68

STRENGTH

He gives strength to the weary,
and to him who lacks might He increases power.
ISAIAH 40:29 NASB

There is a fable about a lion and a mouse. The lion has a thorn in his paw, and the tiny mouse—who seemed so helpless a moment before—is able to remove the terrible thorn to make the lion well.

We are less than even mice before God! But God loves to use us as partners in His kingdom business. He creates roles for us to play and listens when we speak. He lets us try out our ideas. The God of the universe—the Lion of Judah—allows us to help Him in his work!

You may feel too weak. Well, yes, you are! But His power is all you need to do miraculous things.

Storms make trees take deeper roots.
DOLLY PARTON, SINGER

GOD'S PROMISES
ABOUT STRENGTH

But the people who know their God
will be strong and will resist him.
DANIEL 11:32 NLT

God is my protection.
He makes my way free from fault.
II SAMUEL 22:33 NCV

The LORD is my strength and my song;
He has become my salvation.
EXODUS 15:2 HCSB

My grace is all you need.
My power works best in weakness.
II CORINTHIANS 12:9 NLT

Have faith in the LORD your God,
and you will stand strong.
Have faith in His prophets,
and you will succeed.
II CHRONICLES 20:20 NCV

69

STRESS AND REST

*His peace will keep your thoughts and your hearts
quiet and at rest as you trust in Christ Jesus.*
PHILIPPIANS 4:7 TLB

In this demanding and distracting world, rest is so important. But many people aren't sure how to rest in a way that fills and refreshes them.

Resting in Jesus isn't too unlike resting on a beach, in a hammock, with a cool glass of water and a good book in hand. Your mind releases its worries—to Jesus. Your body relaxes, as if wrapped in strong arms. Your thoughts turn to all the good qualities of the One who loves you more than anything.

Resting in Jesus can happen at the office or at home, in nature or on a busy street. It's a deliberate, wonderful art form that can revolutionize a person's ability to thrive.

*There's a difference between changing and being
changed...moving and being moved...transforming
and being transformed. The beautiful resting place of
the Lord is to trust Him to do the work while we gaze
in wonder at His beauty.*
TRIESTE VAILLANCOURT, AUTHOR

GOD'S PROMISES ABOUT STRESS AND REST

*The beloved of the L*ORD *shall dwell in safety by Him,*
who shelters him all the day long;
and he shall dwell between His shoulders.
DEUTERONOMY 33:12 NKJV

Come to Me, all of you who are weary
and carry heavy burdens, and I will give you rest.
MATTHEW 11:28 NLT

I find rest in God; only He gives me hope.
PSALM 62:5 NCV

*You, L*ORD*, give true peace to those who depend on You,*
because they trust You.
ISAIAH 26:3 NCV

Pray this way for kings and all who are in authority
so that we can live peaceful and quiet lives
marked by godliness and dignity.
I TIMOTHY 2:2 NLT

70

THANKSGIVING

*Rejoice always, pray without ceasing,
in everything give thanks; for this is the will of God
in Christ Jesus for you.*
I THESSALONIANS 5:16–18 NKJV

Many times in Scripture we're told not to worry. *But,* someone might say, *that must not apply in my current situation. If I don't find a job soon, I don't know what I'll do...or...Mom has cancer, and we don't know if treatments are working....* Worrying must count for something...right?!

But when God says "don't," He means it. That may feel defeating. But it should empower you! He never asks us to do what we can't without His help.

The next time you are prone to worry, be very deliberate about choosing thanks. Think of crazy things to be thankful for. Your dining room table! Boxed hair color! Your boyfriend's knack for gift-giving! Thanks is sometimes the best warfare and always the best lifestyle.

Gratitude turns what we have into enough.
ANONYMOUS

GOD'S PROMISES ABOUT THANKSGIVING

Every morning tell Him,
"Thank You for Your kindness,"
and every evening rejoice in all His faithfulness.
PSALM 92:2 TLB

Enter into His gates with thanksgiving,
and into His courts with praise.
Be thankful to Him, and bless His name.
For the LORD is good; His mercy is everlasting,
and His truth endures to all generations.
PSALM 100:4–5 NKJV

And whatever you do, in word or in deed,
do everything in the name of the Lord Jesus,
giving thanks to God the Father through Him.
COLOSSIANS 3:17 HCSB

Surely the righteous shall give thanks to Your name;
the upright shall dwell in Your presence.
PSALM 140:13 NKJV

Thank God for this gift, His gift.
No language can praise it enough!
II CORINTHIANS 9:15 THE MESSAGE

71

TRUSTING GOD

Trust in the LORD with all your heart;
do not depend on your own understanding.
PROVERBS 3:5 NLT

Some see God's warnings as harsh and demanding. But consider His cautions as extremely helpful information.

God does not vengefully say, "If you trust in people instead of Me, I'm going to curse you, you rotten traitor!" He says, "Be careful because I want you to know this. If you trust in people, it will lead to brokenness."

Likewise, God does not bribe us by saying, "If you choose Me, I'll give you all kinds of sweets!" Instead, He says, "Listen carefully, because I want you to know this. If you trust Me, you'll feel a major difference. You'll learn over time what a true Partner and Friend I am to those who love Me."

Never be afraid to trust an unknown future
to a known God.
CORRIE TEN BOOM, SURVIVOR

GOD'S PROMISES ABOUT TRUSTING HIM

We have depended on God's grace, not on our own human wisdom. That is how we have conducted ourselves before the world.
II CORINTHIANS 1:12 NLT

All God's words are right,
and everything He does is worthy of our trust.
PSALM 33:4 TLB

Trust should be in the living God who always richly gives us all we need for our enjoyment.
I TIMOTHY 6:17 TLB

If you want favor with both God and man,
and a reputation for good judgment
and common sense, then trust the Lord completely;
don't ever trust yourself.
PROVERBS 3:4 TLB

In quietness and trust is your strength.
ISAIAH 30:15 NASB

72

VALUES

Moral character makes for smooth traveling;
an evil life is a hard life.
PROVERBS 11:5 THE MESSAGE

God's values tend to be quite different from our own. Consider the widow who could afford to put one single coin in the offering box. Jesus called her the most generous woman on earth! Her heart was wealthy, even if her pocketbook was empty.

God's idea of success isn't always the top rung of the corporate ladder or the best voice in the talent show. He looks at us from the inside out and loves seeing our motivations in line with His own.

Before you begin your next venture, decide up front with the Lord what success will look like. It may not be money or fame; instead, it may be having fun, loving well, or giving it your very best.

When you live in the light of eternity,
your values change.
RICK WARREN, PASTOR

GOD'S PROMISES
ABOUT VALUES

Because of this, I always try to maintain
a clear conscience before God and all people.
ACTS 24:16 NLT

Let us come near to God with a sincere heart
and a sure faith, because we have been made free
from a guilty conscience, and our bodies
have been washed with pure water.
HEBREWS 10:22 NCV

If then you were raised with Christ,
seek those things which are above,
where Christ is, sitting at the right hand of God.
Set your mind on things above,
not on things on the earth.
COLOSSIANS 3:1-2 NKJV

Fix your attention on God. You'll be changed
from the inside out. Readily recognize what He wants
from you, and quickly respond to it. Unlike the
culture around you, always dragging you down to its
level of immaturity, God brings the best out of you,
develops well-formed maturity in you.
ROMANS 12:2 THE MESSAGE

The integrity of the upright guides them,
but the perversity of the treacherous destroys them.
PROVERBS 11:3 HCSB

73

WISDOM AND UNDERSTANDING

For the LORD grants wisdom!
From His mouth come knowledge and understanding.
He grants a treasure of common sense to the honest.
He is a shield to those who walk with integrity.
PROVERBS 2:6-7 NLT

The elderly are full of rich wisdom. Their experience on earth surpasses any other people you interact with on a daily basis. They may not always recognize it—but the elderly are treasure troves of stories, examples, and advice for younger people.

Not many folks love wrinkles and saggy skin. But the Lord appreciates the wisdom that wrinkles represent. Proverbs 16:31 makes that clear, calling gray hair a crown of glory coming from a godly life.

If you are close to a grandparent or a friend who is a couple generations above you, consider yourself blessed. They are beautiful and full of wisdom that grows every day.

The more wisdom enters our hearts, the more we will
be able to trust our hearts in difficult situations.
JOHN ELDREDGE, AUTHOR

GOD'S PROMISES ABOUT WISDOM AND UNDERSTANDING

It's better to be wise than strong;
intelligence outranks muscle any day.
PROVERBS 24:5 THE MESSAGE

Never walk away from Wisdom—she guards your life;
love her—she keeps her eye on you.
PROVERBS 4:6 THE MESSAGE

Those who are wise will shine as bright as the sky,
and those who lead many to righteousness
will shine like the stars forever.
DANIEL 12:3 NLT

Get wisdom—how much better it is than gold!
And get understanding—it is preferable to silver.
PROVERBS 16:16 HCSB

But the wisdom that is from above is first pure,
then peaceable, gentle, willing to yield,
full of mercy and good fruits,
without partiality and without hypocrisy.
JAMES 3:17 NKJV

74

WORK AND
DEDICATION

*Work willingly at whatever you do, as though you
were working for the Lord rather than for people.*
COLOSSIANS 3:23 NLT

What martial artist do you know who, at his
very first tournament as a novice, steps into
the ring with a champion black-belt fighter and
wins? Nobody! It takes years of dedication and training to excel to the point of champion. How many
Olympic athletes get to the games in the first year of
their sport?

Training is an absolute necessity for anyone
wanting to succeed. It is the same for every believer.
We need knowledge and understanding. Practice
succeeding, and practice failing. Direction from God
and from trusted friends. We need work!

Train hard with the Word and with the Holy
Spirit and you will have favor in whatever you choose
to work at.

I want to run every race with a big heart.
RYAN HALL, ATHLETE

GOD'S PROMISES ABOUT WORK AND DEDICATION

Lazy people are soon poor; hard workers get rich.
A wise youth harvests in the summer.
PROVERBS 10:4–5 NLT

Cynics look high and low for wisdom—and never find
it; the open-minded find it right on their doorstep!
PROVERBS 14:6 THE MESSAGE

But this I say: he who sows sparingly
will also reap sparingly, and he who sows bountifully
will also reap bountifully.
II CORINTHIANS 9:6 NKJV

Be strong and courageous, and do the work.
Don't be afraid or discouraged, for the LORD God,
my God is with you. He won't leave you
or forsake you.
I CHRONICLES 28:20 HCSB

The plans of hard-working people earn a profit,
but those who act too quickly become poor.
PROVERBS 21:5 NCV

75

WORSHIP

God is spirit, and those who worship Him must worship in spirit and truth.
JOHN 4:24 HCSB

Worship is more than songs on a Sunday morning. Worship is a lifestyle, meant to be lived by every single believer—whether or not they can sing!

Worship is a response to His holiness. And in order to be able to respond to something, a person needs to experience it first. First, we seek, observe, and immerse ourselves in His truth. That can be at church or in the Word, in the forest or on a mountain, or in a conversation with your best friend. Once we experience His presence, it moves us. And we worship Him.

Don't wait for a Sunday morning to "sing praise and worship." Seek out His holiness in life now. Like, right now. And respond as you are led.

Worship is simply giving God His breath back.
LOUIE GIGLIO, PASTOR

GOD'S PROMISES
ABOUT WORSHIP

I was glad when they said to me,
"Let us go into the house of the Lord."
PSALM 122:1 NKJV

Happy are those who hear the joyful call to worship,
for they will walk in the light of Your presence, Lord.
PSALM 89:15 NLT

All the earth will worship You and sing praise to You.
They will sing praise to Your name.
PSALM 66:4 HCSB

For where two or three are gathered together
in My name, I am there among them.
MATTHEW 18:20 HCSB

Worship the Lord with gladness. Come before Him,
singing with joy. Acknowledge that the Lord is God!
He made us, and we are His. We are His people,
the sheep of His pasture.
PSALM 100:2–3 NLT

LIVE YOUR FAITH

Dear Friend,

This book was prayerfully crafted with you, the reader, in mind—every word, every sentence, every page—was thoughtfully written, designed, and packaged to encourage you... right where you are this very moment. At DaySpring, our vision is to see every person experience the life-changing message of God's love. So, as we worked through rough drafts, design changes, edits, and details, we prayed for you to deeply experience His unfailing love, indescribable peace, and pure joy. It is our sincere hope that through these Truth-filled pages your heart will be blessed, knowing that God cares about you—your desires and disappointments, your challenges and dreams.

He knows. He cares. He loves you unconditionally.

BLESSINGS!
THE DAYSPRING BOOK TEAM

Additional copies of this book and
other DaySpring titles can be purchased
at fine bookstores everywhere.
Order online at <u>dayspring.com</u>
or
by phone at 1-877-751-4347